Penguin Handbooks

Whole Earth Cookbook

D1362583

Sharon Cadwallader and Judi Ohr run the Whole Earth
Restaurant on the campus of the University of
California at Santa Cruz. Opened in 1970, this now
famous restaurant is a non-profitmaking concern,
devoted entirely to 'natural foods' and staffed by
students.

Sharon Cadwallader is a long-time devotee of 'natural
food' cooking and manager of the Whole Earth
Restaurant. Born in Jamestown, North Dakota, in
1936, she graduated from San José State College in
1958, has been a school teacher, and is currently living
in Santa Cruz, where she teaches English to
foreign-born residents. She has one son.

Judi Ohr, who developed the bread and dessert recipes
in this book, comes from a Sicilian family of excellent
cooks, and was born and raised in a farming community
near San José. She has two children.

Sharon Cadwallader and Judi Ohr

Whole Earth Cookbook

*Recipes tested in the Whole Earth Restaurant
on the University of California Campus,
Santa Cruz, California*

Preface by Paul Lee

Illustrated by Anita Walker Scott

Penguin Books
in association with
André Deutsch

Penguin Books Ltd, Harmondsworth,
Middlesex, England
Penguin Books Australia Ltd, Ringwood,
Victoria, Australia

First published in the U.S.A. by Houghton Mifflin 1972
Published in Great Britain by André Deutsch
(hardback) and Penguin Books 1973
Copyright © San Francisco Book Co. Inc., 1972

Made and printed in Great Britain by
Hazell Watson & Viney Ltd, Aylesbury Bucks
Set in Monotype Plantin

Although the Whole Earth Restaurant is located on the campus of the
University of California in Santa Cruz, it is a private, non-profit
organization and in no way is *Whole Earth Cookbook* an official
publication of the University of California

THIS BOOK IS DEDICATED TO A HEALTHY, HAPPY
WHOLE EARTH

With love and gratitude to
the Whole Earth Restaurant family: Jane, Linda, Rock,
Cathy, Tom, Nick, Carol, Bonnie, Gene, Karen,
Paul, Ed, Herb, Jerry, Charlene, Bill,
Bob, and Jay, and the Staff of Life Bakery;
and special thanks to Jeanne for her help in editing,
typing, and assembling.

Contents

Foreword to the British Edition

The past few years in the United States have brought about a great commitment to better nutrition and food preparation. This is a direct result of the controversies over chemical sprays and pesticides used in the raising of commercial produce and the sizeable increase in technological foods (those ingredients that have undergone high heating and chemical processing to produce 'instant' foods). What is significant about this movement is that it is really a rebirth of wholesome American farm cooking rather than an indulgence in health food faddism.

Undoubtedly this same phenomenon is occurring in most technological countries especially among the young. We feel that *Whole Earth Cook Book* can provide ideas and insights that will be beneficial to the diets of our international friends. The British have long been praised for their solid country cooking, which is a valid basis for the return to simple, healthful foods. We urge everyone to be as free and creative as they wish with these recipes, and to substitute and experiment to satisfy their own tastes. It is not only the poet, but the cook who deserves licence.

Best wishes,

Sharon Cadwallader
Judi Ohr

Preface

When Stuart Brand first told me about the significance of the first photograph, from outer space, of the whole earth, I didn't understand him. But I pondered it in my heart. When Stuart and Lois came through northern Wisconsin and stopped at Cisco Point, on their first Whole Earth Truck Tour, I had a little better idea of what was going down. I bought a tipi. Now that the *Whole Earth Catalog* has come and gone the message is clear.

The Whole Earth came into perspective with the photograph of the whole earth. Now every point is equidistant from every other point, as every person is equidistant from every other person. The coincidence of opposites, prophesied by that wonderful old Christian, Nicolaus Cusanus, has become a reality. The responsibility for nurturing and transforming the Whole Earth is up to us; we are in it together to get it together, to realize in ourselves, with one another, the Whole Earth.

There are two pieces of earth where this effort is taking place, both of them at the University of California, Santa Cruz. One is on a slope at the upper entrance of the University – the Student Garden Project. Dedicated to the memories of Von Moltke and Bonhoeffer, the Garden is the transition from the holocaust to the Whole Earth. Dedicated to biodynamic, organic, vitalist, ecological horticulture, the Garden, under the mastership of Alan Chadwick, is a model of that community of wholesomeness the vision of the Whole Earth means to nurture and foster.

Whole

(1) Possessing, or being in, a state of health and soundness; well; sound; hence, healed.

(2) Not broken; unimpaired; integral, as in integrated, self-integration.

(3) Containing the total amount, number; complete; entire; intact; perfect.

On another slope, as an outgrowth of the Student Garden, the Whole Earth Restaurant is dedicated to the new sensibility of the Whole Earth and the restoration of kinship with the Whole Earth. Situated midway between the Wilderness and the Garden, the Whole Earth Restaurant takes part in that exodus from institutional bondage we are all called upon to enact; this *Whole Earth Cook Book* provides you with the recipes for doing it yourself as one of us.

21 July, 1971   *Paul Lee*
Cisco Point
Phelps, Wisconsin

Introduction

What are natural foods?

For many years nutritionists have been lecturing about the deficiencies in our national diet, but their audience has been very small and little of this information ever filtered through to the large middle segment of our population. However, in the last two or three years more and more people have become aware of the need for change in their nutritional patterns. Many of the younger generation have taken the responsibility of altering their diets and are converting to pure foods with the zeal of atonement. Numerous articles have been published in magazines and newspapers about the overrefinement of grain products, excessive consumption of sugar and saturated fats, and the amount of chemical additives in prepared foods. Public controversy over the indiscriminate use of pesticides and chemical fertilizers in farming initiated research in the danger of these chemicals to human life. The results were alarming and the U.S. government has begun to abolish the use of some of the more lethal sprays.

What do all the changes signify?

Let us start at the beginning. It is a basic biological fact that no plant can be superior to the soil in which it was grown. If, after each growing season, the unused vegetation is removed from the ground that nourished it, rather than retained to decompose naturally to feed the next crop, all the important vitamins and minerals will soon disappear from the soil. This is what is happening to the large commercial farming areas of

America. In order to increase the growing periods, each crop is being fed with chemical stimulants and fertilizers, yet each year tons of unused produce are discarded or dumped in the ocean to maintain high consumer prices. The economics are inefficient and our health is in jeopardy.

Unfortunately, there are other areas of gross negligence in our food raising. The modern feedlot techniques of the large meat producers are so unhealthy that one cattleman commented to us, 'I raise a private stock for my own use.' But, until the consumer demands natural raising of meat and insists that the government forbid the injecting of chemicals and ban the use of poisons and waste in animal feed, these practices will continue. At the present time the most you can do for your diet is to select the best cuts from a clean butcher's shop. Avoid packaged-meat counters and do not buy prepared luncheon meats because of the questionable ingredients and chemical additives. Learn to cook offal, such as liver, kidney, and sweetbreads, and the less common muscle sections, like tongue and heart. These parts of the animal are the richest in B vitamins and are cheaper than the standard cuts. Also, in some areas of the country, you can buy naturally fed meats which are not injected with chemicals. We suggest you inquire about the availability of organic meats in your area.

Chicken farmers are also guilty of malpractice in the mass production of chickens for consumption. In fact, last year California passed a law forbidding the injection of chickens with antibiotics, so gross were the results of this practice. Chickens raised on natural feeds and allowed the freedom to scratch taste much better than those who spend their lives with thousands of other chickens jammed in a building and fed nothing short of trash. Laying hens that are raised under these conditions, and without a rooster, produce eggs lacking in important hormones, enzymes, and protein found in fertilized eggs.

Along with these concerns is the condition of the freshwater fish in the United States. So much industrial waste is dumped into our rivers and lakes that there are places where no fish is safe to be eaten. Even salt water in some of the coastal areas is so polluted that the fish are toxic. Today it is wisest to buy bottom and deep-sea fish.

Another major source of nutrition which needs improvement is the dairy industry. Though it is not quite as careless in its practices, yet there is still the question of preservatives added to milk and milk products. At the same time, the pasteurization process causes a reduction in the amount of calcium and the destruction of hormones and enzymes. Raw milk and raw milk products are the best sources of these nutrients, providing – and this is important – the milk comes from a clean, certified herd and is handled very carefully. There are few of these herds in the country, so you will probably have to continue using pasteurized milk for now. Try to find a local dairy, though, and check their practices.

There have already been many articles published about the enormous intake of sugar in the United States. A few of our recipes call for natural sugar, but we think natural sugars are mainly a psychological comfort – they look natural. We urge substitution of uncooked, unfiltered honeys for sugar whenever possible. We also recommend the use of sea salt to avoid the chemicals in ordinary table salt.

Natural foods, then, are simply those vegetables, fruits, and grains which are grown in soils rich in organic matter, without chemical treatment, and those animals that are raised on natural feeds and allowed to move freely in healthy pastures. It is not the basic ingredients of our diet which are in question, but the quality of these ingredients does invite criticism. We do not need a larger variety of foodstuffs, more attractive packaging, larger economy sizes, pretty, symmetrical produce. We need nutritional quality. If we are made aware of the total cycle of the food we eat, we will become more conscious of its quality.

We urge you to pressure local farmers to return to organic gardening methods, and to demand that natural products be stocked on supermarket shelves, and that harmful and nutritionless foods be removed. For many years the so-called health food store held a mystique alien to most Americans. Now, all over the country, natural food stores are springing up full of products we will be discussing in this book. More natural grains and flours are appearing in the big supermarkets. We are very optimistic.

We hope the following recipes will stimulate your interest in planning a healthy diet. Do not discard your favourite recipes; instead, substitute natural ingredients and prepare your foods carefully to guard against the loss of nutrients. None of our recipes is complicated, as we want to turn you on to the relaxation in simple, natural cooking. The country kitchen is a traditional gathering place. Let this style pull you into the fun of cooking. We at the Whole Earth Restaurant make a party out of preparing meals. We hope you will do the same with your family and friends, and that every day brings another party.

Soups

A French friend once lamented, 'How will my poor child ever adjust to these canned soups in the United States?' To Americans a fine soup is identified with an exceptionally fine cook, but to the French making good soup is assumed. In actuality there are only a few tricks and, with a little knowledge and a minimum of effort, you can prepare a delicious soup every time.

One secret is the stock. In all your food preparations keep the soup stock in a corner of your kitchen thoughts. Vegetable cooking water should be saved and refrigerated. If you have access to fresh organic vegetables, save parings, scraps, pits, seeds, outer lettuce leaves and fertile-egg shells. (Commercial eggs are often sprayed with disinfectants.) Put them in a bag or container in the refrigerator until you have enough to make a good stock, about 1 or 2 pounds. Dump them in a large pot with 2 or 3 pints of water and simmer, covered, for 30–45 minutes. Strain and store stock in refrigerator.

Learn to recycle scraps into the next soup. All leftovers – meat, vegetables, salads, grains, eggs, cheese, even bread – can be added to soup. We are including a recipe for making meat stock which can be frozen or refrigerated for later use (see below). When you are sprouting seeds (see page 17) be sure to save the sprout water for stock. You can make wonderful soups very quickly if you have a good, hearty stock.

When preparing soup, add the vegetables in the last stage so the vitamins and minerals do not evaporate in cooking. If you are using a vegetable stock without meat, it is best to sauté some of the vegetables before adding them to the stock. This helps to hold the flavour in the vegetable, and the oil or butter adds richness to the soup. If a stock needs a tomato touch, we have found that the best results are obtained by adding V-8 juice rather than tomato juice, along with fresh tomatoes if you wish.

A hearty soup served with whole-grain bread and a vegetable salad is a very satisfying meal.

Meat Soup Stock

Some butcher's shops give marrow bones and chicken feet away. Soup bones are always very cheap. Use young beef or veal bones; ribs, back, shoulder, or any marrow bone will make good jelly stock. Oxtail and shin cost more but have good flavour for minestrone. Use chicken feet or backs if available.

Simmer bones together with 2 or 3 pints of water, depending on the amount of bones, and 3 tablespoons vinegar, 2 bay leaves, salt and pepper. Simmer, covered, about 3 hours. Remove any meat and discard bones. Chill stock and skim off any excess fat. Freeze if desired.

Cheese Soybean Soup

Follow directions for cooking soybeans in Basic Soybean Recipe (see page 38).

Mash soybeans with 1 large can of V-8 juice. You can use a blender. Place them in a soup pot.

Sauté and add to soup:

3 tablespoons oil
1 small onion, chopped
1 clove garlic, mashed

2 stalks chopped celery, both stalks and leaves

Add:

6 oz grated cheese, preferably Cheddar

Simmer for 30 minutes and season to taste. Serves 5 to 6.

Onion Soup

2 oz butter or margarine
3 large onions, sliced
3 tablespoons flour
½ pint rich chicken broth

¾ pint rich beef broth
1 pint water
2 oz grated Parmesan cheese

Heat butter and sauté onions until golden and tender. Sprinkle with flour. Gradually stir in chicken and beef broth and water. Simmer, stirring occasionally, for 15 minutes or until onions are tender. Sprinkle with cheese. Salt may be added. Serves 5 to 6.

Easy Oyster or Clam Chowder

2 rashers bacon, chopped
1 small onion, chopped
2 stalks celery, chopped
1½ pints water
3 potatoes, cut up
3 carrots, cut up

1 (10-ounce) can oysters or clams
salt and pepper
½ teaspoon each of dried thyme, tarragon, and oregano
½ pint single cream

Cook bacon until soft; then add onion and celery and sauté together. Meanwhile, put water in soup pot and simmer potatoes and carrots. When nearly tender add oysters or clams (include liquid), salt, pepper, thyme, tarragon, and oregano. Simmer 10 minutes. Add the sautéed bacon and vegetables. Just before serving (off fire), add the cream. Heat through without boiling. Serves 4 to 5 depending on appetite.

Variation: For Manhattan-style chowder add 1 (12-ounce) can V-8 juice together with clams or oysters. Caraway seeds may be added.

Split Pea Soup with Ham Hock

½ ham hock   1 small onion, chopped
¼ teaspoon dried savory   salt and pepper
1 clove garlic, mashed

Follow the directions for Split Pea-Vegetable Stew (see page 42); however, after peas have cooked 1 hour add the ingredients above.

Simmer, covered, for 1½ to 2 more hours. Add more water if too thick. Caraway seeds may be added before serving. Serves 5 to 6.

Vegetable Minsetrone

3 pints vegetable cooking water   1 (15-ounce) can kidney beans
4 oz barley   and liquid, or cooked
1 large onion, sliced   equivalent
3 tablespoons chopped fresh   3 or 4 carrots, sliced thin
  parsley   1 stalk celery, chopped
2 cloves garlic, mashed   ½ teaspoon dried oregano
3 tablespoons oil   1 bay leaf
1 (14-ounce) can tomatoes   salt and pepper
1 (12-ounce) can V-8 juice   3 tablespoons red wine
1 lb lima beans, cooked and
  mashed

Bring water to the boil; add barley and simmer until tender, 45 minutes to 1 hour. Meanwhile sauté onion, parsley, and garlic in oil. Mix all ingredients in soup pot and simmer, covered, for 1 to 1½ hours. Before serving add 3 tablespoons red wine. Serve with grated Parmesan. Serves 6 to 8.

Optional addition: cooked whole-wheat or soy macaroni may be added in the last half-hour.

Spanish Gazpacho

1½ pints chicken broth,
  chilled
2 tablespoons olive oil
8 tablespoons lime juice
3 or 4 tomatoes, diced

1 onion, diced
2 large green peppers, diced
1 stalk celery, diced
dash of Tabasco sauce

Mix all the ingredients together. Vegetables must be diced fine. Add Tabasco sauce to taste. Chill thoroughly before serving. Serves 6.

Spinach Soup

1½ pints salted water
1½ lb spinach, chopped

2 tablespoons oil
1 medium onion, thinly sliced

Bring water to the boil, add spinach, and simmer for 5 to 7 minutes. Meanwhile, in the oil, sauté the onions until they are clear. Add them to the spinach together with:

¼ pint single cream or milk
1 teaspoon curry powder, or
  to taste

4 oz cooked rice, barley,
  potatoes, or any leftover
  grain

Salt to taste and heat thoroughly. Serve with lemon wedges. Serves 4 to 6.

Green Soup

Simmer for 20 minutes in ¾ pint water:

3 tablespoons diced green   2 tablespoons chopped onion
  pepper
10 oz chopped broccoli

Next, mix these vegetables well in the blender until they are puréed. Place in a soup pot and add:

1 tablespoon butter   ¼ pint buttermilk
½ pint single cream or milk   ½ teaspoon curry powder
salt to taste

Heat through and serve. This is also delicious served cold with lemon. Serves 4.

Cabbage-Potato Borscht

In a large soup pot, cook until tender with salt and pepper in 1½ pints vegetable cooking water:

1 medium onion, sliced   1 small cabbage, shredded

Meanwhile, in another pot, cook in 1½ pints vegetable cooking water:

3 or 4 potatoes, diced   4 or 5 carrots, diced

When tender, drain potato water into cabbage broth. Mash potatoes and carrots together with:

½ pint sour cream   1 teaspoon dried dill
                                    (optional)

Next, add the sour-cream mixture to the broth, very slowly to avoid curdling. Stir continually during this part. Add more salt and pepper to taste. Serve immediately.

Pumpkin-Mushroom Soup

½ lb mushrooms, sliced
1 medium onion, chopped
2 tablespoons butter or oil
2 tablespoons flour
1 tablespoon curry powder
1¼ pints chicken broth

1 lb pumpkin
1 tablespoon honey
dash of nutmeg
salt and pepper
½ pint milk

Sauté mushrooms and onion in butter or oil. Add flour and curry and stir. Gradually add broth. Add everything but the milk and cook, stirring, for 10 to 15 minutes. Add milk and heat through without boiling. May be topped with sour cream or yogurt (see page 42). Serves 6.

Fresh Cream of Tomato Soup

3 pints water or vegetable
   cooking water
3 or 4 bouillon cubes,
   vegetable or chicken
1 large onion, chopped
10 to 12 medium tomatoes,
   peeled and chopped
6 stalks celery, chopped

1 teaspoon salt
3 or 4 tablespoons honey
2 tablespoons butter
1 teaspoon paprika
½ pint milk and ¼ pint single
   cream

Bring water to boil. Add bouillon cubes, vegetables, and salt. Simmer 30 minutes. Transfer to blender and mix well. Add honey, butter, and paprika. Return to pan and add milk and cream slowly to prevent curdling. Heat through and serve. Serves 6 to 8.

Haricot Bean Soup

Cook 1 lb haricot beans according to the Basic Bean Recipe (see page 36). Meanwhile, in 5 or 6 tablespoons of olive oil, sauté:

2 large onions, sliced   3 oz fresh, chopped parsley
2 garlic cloves, crushed

Combine this with the beans and add:

½ teaspoon dried thyme   2 tablespoons salt
¼ cup tomato paste   pepper
juice of ½ lemon

Simmer for 30 minutes. Serves 8.

Salads
and Vegetables

SALADS. In this era of organicity, of vegetarian diets and home gardening, we find an increasing interest in the preparation of fresh and cooked vegetables. Included in this section are a few hints to help give more nutrition and enjoyment to this part of your diet. Given the vast selection of fresh vegetables on the market today, the traditional lettuce, tomato and cucumber salad are relatively unimaginative. Also, the variety of vegetables being frozen each year increases and during the winter season, when fresh vegetables are not easily obtainable, you can defrost some of these vegetables and use them in fresh salads.

In preparing salads, we urge you to use as many raw vegetables and fruits as are available. Use a vegetable brush and scrub root vegetables. Wash green, leafy vegetables quickly and dry them well. Do not soak vegetables, because many nutrients will be released into the water. When trying new vegetables in a salad, grate them or slice them very thin. When using greens new to you, chop fine and use the young leaves. Combine fruits and vegetables together. Experiment and find your favourites. Along with lettuce, tomatoes, avocados, onions, and cucumbers, you can use:

parsley	broccoli and cauliflower
kale	leaves
chicory	raw cauliflower and broccoli
turnip tops	young nasturtium leaves

spinach

cabbages (Chinese, Savoy)

endive

beet tops

Swiss chard

dandelion greens
  (slightly bitter)

young peas with pod

young milkweed leaves
  (grow wild)

any root vegetables (beets,
  turnips, parsnips, etc.)

alfalfa or mung-bean
  sprouts

Fresh sprouts are a superb source of vitamins, five times higher than the seed-grain form. Any seed, whole grain, dried pea, or dried bean, can be sprouted. Alfalfa and mung bean are the most frequently sold. (See page 17 for instructions for sprouting seeds.)

Additional suggestions:

grated cheese

chopped hard-boiled eggs

chopped nuts

sunflower, pumpkin, poppy,
  or sesame seeds

We include a recipe for a basic dressing, a yogurt dressing, and a delicious mayonnaise from which you can make your own favourite cream dressings.

VEGETABLES. There are two important rules for cooking vegetables: (1) wash well, but do not soak, and (2) do not overcook. If anything, vegetables should be undercooked. They should be firm, and the stems of green leafy vegetables should be slightly crisp. The easiest way to avoid overcooking vegetables is to buy a vegetable steamer. We recommend the stainless-steel variety, which is collapsible and fits any pot. Besides losing fewer nutrients in the water, you will find the taste fresher and better. The water you use under the steamer should be retained and refrigerated for use in soups or cooking grains. It is nice to add a little oil, garlic, and herbs while steaming. Salt just before serving. Another good way to prepare vegetables is in an Oriental manner. Chop the vegetables into equal-sized pieces. Sauté the vegetables in a heavy skillet in a little oil. Reduce the heat to the lowest point, cover, and steam briefly.

Herbs and garlic on vegetables will turn your taste around. Vegetables are the best reason for raising herbs. Even if you live in the city, you can plant herbs in flowerpots or in the centre of cement blocks. If you do not have access to fresh herbs, the dried variety can be substituted as long as you remember to use one half the amount required for fresh herbs.

Spinach Salad

1½ lb freshly picked spinach
½ onion, sliced
2 hard-boiled eggs, diced
2 tablespoons vegetable oil

4 tablespoons wine vinegar
4 tablespoons water
1 teaspoon salt
½ teaspoon pepper

Clean spinach carefully, as each leaf can hold dirt. Place clean, washed leaves in a bowl and add the onion and eggs. Mix together oil, vinegar, water, salt, and pepper. Pour over the salad and toss lightly.

Super Caesar Salad

5 tablespoons salad oil
1 garlic clove, minced
4 slices bread, crusts removed
    and cubed
1 large cos lettuce
1 large endive
1 oz grated Parmesan cheese

2 oz crumbled blue cheese
3 tablespoons lemon juice
¼ teaspoon Tabasco sauce
¾ teaspoon salt
¼ teaspoon dry mustard
1 raw egg

Heat 2 tablespoons of salad oil and garlic in a frying pan. Add the bread cubes and sauté until lightly browned. Remove and set aside. Tear crisp, chilled lettuce into bite-sized pieces and place in a salad bowl. Sprinkle with Parmesan and blue cheese. Combine the rest of the salad oil, and the lemon juice, Tabasco sauce, salt, and dry mustard, and shake to blend. Pour over the salad greens and toss lightly. Then break the egg into salad greens and toss lightly until the egg particles disappear. Add the croûtons and again toss lightly. Serves 6.

Lemon Bean Salad

1 lb dried white beans	3 tablespoons olive oil
3 tablespoons lemon juice	2 cloves garlic, minced
½ teaspoon pepper	1 small lettuce, shredded
3 tablespoons chopped chives	

Cook beans as directed in the Basic Bean Recipe (see page 36). Mix together all the remaining ingredients. Beat well and pour over the beans. Chill thoroughly.

Special Summer Salad

1 pineapple	6 oz grapes
6 apricots, cut up	4 oz shredded coconut
1 banana, sliced	(preferably unsweetened)
½ cantaloupe, or other	1 pint sour cream
melon, diced	1 oz chopped walnuts

Chill pineapple overnight. Slice in half. Cut out core and then cut out pineapple. Put in bowl along with other cut-up fruit. Add coconut, sour cream, and nuts. Mix well. Chill until ready to serve.

Cheese and Courgette Salad

2 hard-boiled eggs, chopped
2 medium courgettes, grated
1 small lettuce, shredded
garlic salt

1 small onion, thinly sliced
¼ lb grated cheese
salt, pepper and dill
Basic Dressing (see page 19)

Combine all ingredients, adding salt, pepper, dill, garlic salt, and Basic Dressing to taste. Toss lightly.

Caraway Cabbage Salad

½ medium-sized red cabbage
½ medium-sized green
  cabbage
½ medium onion

Basic Dressing (see page 19)
salt, pepper, and garlic salt
1 teaspoon caraway seeds

Shred and chop cabbage as thin as possible. Slice onion and then pull it apart. Toss with Basic Dressing, salt, pepper, and garlic salt, adding as much of these as desired to satisfy your taste. Add caraway seeds and toss lightly.

Sprouting Seeds

Use approximately 2 tablespoons of seeds, or about 4 tablespoons of legumes. Put your seeds in a quart jar. Cover them with warm water and soak for 8 hours. Drain off the liquid through a cheesecloth or wire mesh which has been placed under the ring of the jar lid. Rinse the seeds and drain them well. Now lay the jar on its side. Rinse the sprouts two or three times a day and place the jar back on its side. Be careful not to let the sprouts set too long in water or dry out, as this will cause the crop to spoil. Within three or four days the sprouts will have developed completely and they will be ready to eat and/or refrigerate.

It is advisable to keep the sprout jar in a dark place (the cupboard) for the first two or three days and bring it out in the light on the last day when the chlorophyll develops. This process generally produces nice green sprouts.

Legumes and seeds for sprouting can be obtained in natural food stores and mills. We particularly recommend using alfalfa seeds because of their delicate taste.

Apple-Raisin Slaw

5–6 oz seedless raisins
rosé wine
1 tablespoon lemon juice
3 apples, diced with their
skin on

½ medium-sized cabbage,
shredded
1 cup mayonnaise (see page
19)

Combine raisins with wine. Cover and let stand several hours or overnight. Sprinkle lemon juice over coarsely diced apples and stir well. Mix with raisins and wine and shredded cabbage. Add the mayonnaise and season to taste. Toss and serve at once. This goes well with ham, roast pork, or turkey. Serves 6 to 8.

Basic Dressing

For a large salad to serve 6 to 8.

3 tablespoons oil
salt, pepper, garlic salt
3 tablespoons lemon juice or
  wine vinegar

herbs and seeds (select from
oregano, basil, tarragon,
thyme, curry powder,
caraway, dill, or sesame
seeds)

1. Be sure that the vegetables are free from water.
2. Sprinkle oil on salad and toss well to coat all the vegetables. Oil holds in the nutrients.
3. Add salt, pepper, garlic salt, herbs and/or seeds, and toss again.
4. Sprinkle in lemon juice or vinegar, toss well, and serve immediately. A dash of soy sauce is nice with lemon dressing.

If this dressing is too tart, decrease the amount of vinegar or lemon. Experiment and find your own taste. Once you get the knack of this method of dressing salads, you will look forward to preparing salads daily.

Mayonnaise

Blend in a blender:

2 egg yolks
½ teaspoon salt
2 tablespoons white-wine
vinegar

2 tablespoons lemon juice
¼ teaspoon dry mustard
dash of cayenne

Next, slowly blend in up to ¾ pint oil, depending on desired thickness. The more oil, the thicker the mayonnaise will be.

Yogurt-Olive Dressing

1 cup yogurt (see page 42)   salt, pepper, garlic powder
½ cup mayonnaise (see above)   dash of Tabasco sauce
4 oz black olives, chopped

Mix all the ingredients well. This dressing is best on heavy
vegetables such as cabbage, beets, carrots, etc.

Vegetable Loaf

1 medium aubergine   ½ teaspoon dried oregano
3–4 stalks celery, diced   1 tablespoon wheat germ
1 medium onion, chopped   1 tablespoon tofu (see page
1 tomato, diced   35)
4 tablespoons butter   garlic powder
1 egg   salt
6 tablespoons bread crumbs   4 tablespoons bread crumbs

Peel and chop aubergine fine, or grind it in a meat or food
grinder. Place in a frying pan, add vegetables, and sauté in
butter. Remove to a mixing bowl and cool. Add egg, breadcrumbs, oregano, wheat germ, tofu, garlic, and salt to taste,
and place in greased baking dish. Sprinkle with remaining
bread crumbs and bake in 350°F, gas 4, preheated oven for 25
minutes.

Note: If tofu (soybean curd) is not available, cottage cheese
can be used.

Spinach or Green Beans with Bacon

1½ lb spinach, or 1½ lb green
  beans
2 rashers of bacon, diced

1 clove garlic, mashed
1 medium onion, sliced
salt and pepper

Wash and chop spinach, or trim beans. In heavy pan, brown
bacon until almost crisp. Add mashed garlic, greens or beans,
and onion, and sauté lightly. Beans may be steamed slightly
first. Cover and reduce heat; steam, turning occasionally until
the leaves of the greens are limp and/or the beans are only
slightly crisp. Add salt and pepper to taste.

Aubergine Pizza

1 medium aubergine, unpeeled
  and sliced thin
¾ pint pizza sauce (page 25)
1 bunch spring onions,
  chopped

2 cloves garlic, mashed
1 teaspoon dried oregano
8 oz grated mozzarella
  cheese
4 oz black olives, sliced

Place aubergine slices in a shallow baking dish. Mix sauce,
onions, garlic, and oregano, and pour evenly over the slices of
aubergine. Top with cheese and olives. Bake at 350°F, gas 4,
for 20 minutes. Eat with a fork. Serves 3 to 4.

Mexican Stuffed Marrow

This is for a large marrow. Simply scale down the recipe for smaller ones.

1 large, 3- to 5-lb marrow	1 can sweet corn
2 rashers bacon, chopped	2 oz black olives, sliced
3 tablespoons chopped green pepper	6 oz cooked rice
1 onion, chopped	1–1¼ pint chili sauce
½ lb mushrooms, chopped	2 eggs, beaten
2 cloves garlic, mashed	salt and pepper
	4 oz grated Parmesan cheese

Slice the marrow lengthwise and scoop the centre out, leaving a shell half an inch thick. If the centre is very pithy, discard it. If it is firm, it can be chopped and combined with the stuffing.

Mix ¾ pint chili sauce with ½ pint water in a large, shallow baking dish. Place both halves of the marrow, skin side down, in the dish, and steam, covered with foil, at 325°F, gas 3, for 30 minutes. Sauté the bacon for 4 to 5 minutes. Then add the pepper, onion, mushrooms, and garlic and cook until onion is clear. Remove. Add corn, olives, rice, the rest of the chili sauce, the beaten eggs, and salt and pepper, and mix all together.

Scoop mixture into the marrow shells; top with the grated cheese. Cover again with foil and bake until marrow shell is tender, to taste, approximately 30 to 45 minutes. Serves 8.

Courgettes with Mushrooms

6 courgettes
½ teaspoon salt
⅛ teaspoon pepper
1 tablespoon butter or
　margarine
1 large onion, chopped

6 tablespoons red wine
½ pint tomato sauce (see
　page 25)
¼ lb fresh mushrooms,
　washed and cut up

Wash courgettes and cut into cubes. In a large saucepan, combine with all remaining ingredients. Simmer slowly until courgettes are just tender (5 to 7 minutes). This is a hearty dish, a good accompaniment to white fish or beef. Serves 3 to 4.

Baked Asparagus Almond

2 lb fresh asparagus
¾ pint white sauce
lemon

dash of Worcester sauce
¼ lb sharp cheese, grated
6 oz blanched almonds

Cook asparagus until just tender. Do not overcook. Make a white sauce and season it with lemon and a dash of Worcester sauce. In a greased casserole arrange alternate layers of asparagus and white sauce to which one half of the grated cheese has been added. Finish with a sprinkle of cheese and the coarsely chopped almonds. Brown lightly in the oven. Serves 5 to 6. (Canned asparagus may be substituted for cooked, fresh asparagus.)

Kale Sauté

2 lb kale
1 large onion, sliced thin
1 clove garlic, mashed

2 tablespoons oil
3 tablespoons prepared
   mustard

Pull kale off the stalk and chop coarsely, saving the stalks for stock. Steam until tender, about 30 minutes. Meanwhile sauté onion and garlic in oil. Add kale to onion and stir in mustard. Serves 4 to 6.

Mushrooms may be added with onion.

Red Cabbage (Sweet and Sour)

1 large head red cabbage
1 tablespoon vegetable oil
6 whole cloves
4 tablespoons honey or 2 oz
   natural sugar
¾ pint red wine vinegar

½ teaspoon cinnamon
1 tablespoon salt
½ teaspoon pepper
2 apples, shredded
2 onions, shredded

Chop the red cabbage, or shred in blender. Place in large pot together with the remaining ingredients. Simmer for approximately 5 hours.

Chived Carrots

5 or 6 medium-sized carrots
2 oz butter or margarine
¼ teaspoon salt

⅛ teaspoon pepper
1 tablespoon snipped chives

Scrub and chop carrots and cook until slightly tender. Melt

butter or margarine. Add carrots, salt, pepper, and snipped chives. Heat until hot and coat with butter. Serves 6.

Tomato Sauce

In blender or electric mixer put:

14 oz drained canned tomatoes	½ teaspoon savory
1 large chopped onion	½ teaspoon mace or nutmeg
6 stalks celery, chopped	½ teaspoon salt
	1 bay leaf

Blend well, put in a saucepan and bring to the boil. Simmer 20 minutes. (Blender or mixer can be eliminated if ingredients are mashed and cooking time is extended 10 minutes.) Run this mixture through a sieve saving the pulp for soup.

Heat 3 tablespoons vegetable oil with 2 tablespoons unbleached flour. Stir in tomato sauce slowly with 1 teaspoon sugar or honey. Simmer and stir as mixture thickens slightly. Makes ¾ pint.

Pizza Sauce

Heat ¾ pint of tomato sauce and stir in 4 oz grated mild cheese and 1 teaspoon oregano.

Chili Sauce

Heat ¾ pint of tomato sauce and stir in 1 teaspoon of chili powder.

Sandwiches

At the Whole Earth Restaurant, we have developed a style of preparing sandwiches where presumption is the first step of preparation. Try anything and everything and, in spite of a few failures, you will have a majority of delicious successes.

We use eggs, scrambled, hard-boiled, and grated; various cheeses, grated; chopped clams, tuna, or shrimps; cottage cheese, cream cheese, or mashed soybeans, in combinations or separately as a base to which we have successfully added parsley, spinach, watercress, onions, alfalfa sprouts, and mushrooms. Sometimes we sauté the vegetables; often we add them raw and chopped fine. We add something crunchy to nearly every sandwich, such as celery, bean sprouts, water chestnuts, sunflower or pumpkin seeds, and ground or chopped nuts of every variety.

Some of the popular sandwiches are: grated egg, ground almond, and green onion; tuna, onion, and sunflower seeds; and grated cheese, sautéed mushrooms, and alfalfa sprouts. It is difficult to give measurements, as we prepare our fillings 'a taste to each step'.

One speciality for which we will include a recipe is our Soybean Spread. You can add to and improve upon this. Try combining it with tuna or egg or cheese.

Soybean Spread

Cook 6 oz soybeans according to the Basic Soybean Recipe (see page 38). When tender, mash well with whatever liquid remains. (They are very hard to mash after refrigeration.) Set aside.

Sauté for 5 minutes:

> 1 large rasher finely chopped bacon

Add and sauté for 5 more minutes:

1 large onion, finely chopped   3 oz fresh, finely chopped
2 cloves garlic, mashed   parsley

Mix sautéed ingredients with the soybeans along with:

1 teaspoon dried oregano   1 tablespoon soy sauce
¾ cup mayonnaise (see page   salt to taste
   19)

Mix thoroughly, using more or less mayonnaise to get the desired consistency for spreading.

Note: Vegetarian bacon bits may be used instead of bacon. If so, then the vegetables should be sautéed in oil, and the bacon bits added last.

Non-meat
Protein Dishes

Nutritional research indicates that the need for protein increases from infancy to age twenty. After twenty the need decreases slightly, except in periods of stress or pregnancy and lactation. Lactation is the time a woman's protein need is greatest.

Briefly, nitrogen-containing amino acids are the essence of protein. These amino acids (twenty-two in all) are vital to the formation and tone of body tissue. Many of these amino acids can be manufactured in the body cells from nitrogen released from other proteins to combine with fat or sugar. Eight cannot be produced by this process and they are referred to as essential amino acids; however, all amino acids are essential to good health. Foods containing these eight amino acids are considered complete proteins. The richest animal sources are egg yolks, milk, and offal, especially liver and kidney.

If one wishes to forgo the eating of animal protein, the utmost care must be given to obtaining protein from alternative foods each day. The best sources, in order of their value, are: soybeans, wheat germ, brewer's yeast, nuts and seeds, and whole grains. Other fair sources are dried beans, peas, and rice. When the diet is without meat, poultry, or fish, but dairy products are eaten occasionally, it is necessary to obtain the purest sources. Milk from a certified dairy or cow is excellent. If it is unavailable, pasteurized or homogenized milk should be fortified with powdered milk. Cheese from unpasteurized milk is delicious, but almost any natural cheese not marked *pro-*

cessed and without additives can be used safely; however, Cheddar and similar cheeses often contain artificial colouring.

Another dairy product, yogurt, is known for its assistance in maintaining essential bacteria in the digestive tract. It has been a staple for many centuries in the Middle Eastern and Balkan countries. We cannot conscientiously recommend using the yogurts sold in supermarkets because of the additives and artificial flavourings. There is also a question involving the value of these cultures. On the other hand, the yogurts sold in natural food stores tend to be expensive when served daily. Therefore, we include a basic recipe for making yogurt.

As mentioned in the Introduction, fertile eggs are an important addition to a good diet. It may take some scouting to find them in the large cities, but results are well worth it.

Whether to use butter or margarine is an issue for the modern cook. Since most margarines contain only slightly less saturated fatty acids than butter, and vitamin A is added to margarine, the choice may be based on the ingredients and taste. Most margarines in supermarkets contain preservatives, so it is wise to read the labels. The natural food stores sell some excellent margarines without chemical additives, which are made from good oils or from soybean extracts.

A description of wheat germ and rice will be found in the discussion of grains on pages 63–5.

Nuts and sunflower, sesame, and pumpkin seeds can be purchased, shelled and unshelled, in natural food stores. High in protein, vitamins, and minerals, they make excellent snacks for children and interesting cooking and baking ingredients. Uncooked nuts, in addition to providing a good source of protein, contain the three essential fatty acids. These are the fatty acids not manufactured by body sugar and are obtained only through food sources. They are also known as unsaturated fatty acids. Their important function is to combine with and transport other nutrients to various parts of the body to build cells. This vital process is inhibited by the adding of hydrogen, which turns fats into solids. Vegetable oils, nuts, and un-hydrogenated nut butters are the best sources of unsaturated fatty acids.

If oils are subject to the high heat of refinement, the vitamin E is lost, and lecithin, a substance essential to the breakdown and absorption of fats, is discarded. When a fat or oil is left unrefrigerated or exposed to oxygen, not only is the vitamin E destroyed, but the oil or fat becomes rancid and destroys the existing vitamin E in the body. Preservatives are added to modern vegetable oils to inhibit rancidity. We suggest using cold-pressed oils which are subjected to less heat in the ex-traction process and are free from preservatives. We prefer safflower for an all-purpose oil. Cold-pressed corn, soy, sesame, and olive oils are also sold in natural food stores.

All dried legumes contain some protein. Split peas, lentils, and haricot, lima, kidney, and pinto beans should be used, along with other protein foods. Soybeans, however, are as high in protein as meat. They are considered a complete protein, or one that contains the eight amino acids. Since they taste different from other legumes and some varieties take more cooking time, they need careful, imaginative preparation. Keep trying to find a recipe that works with your family. They are an outstanding nutritional addition.

Natural food stores carry other soybean products which should be included in a protein-conscious diet. Soy grits, for example, are soybeans broken into small pieces. They are delicious in breads, nut and meat loaves, and casseroles. They should be softened in boiling water for five to ten minutes be-fore use. Another is tofu, or soybean curd or soy cheese. It can be found in Oriental food shops and in natural food stores. Its light, soft consistency and bland taste make it easy to use as an addition or substitute in your favourite recipes. Unfortunately, some tofu brands contain a preservative, so check this when shopping. Soy and/or wheat macaroni noodles are also available and are superior in taste to the bleached flour pasta found everywhere.

Before turning to protein recipes, we should mention nutritional powdered yeasts. Long popular with natural-food enthusiasts, they are specially valuable to people under stress or using a great deal of physical strength. Yeast is a splendid source of B vitamins and minerals. The pick-up can be felt immediately. Unfortunately, the taste is unusual, so it should be introduced in small quantities. Care should be given to selecting the most palatable yeast, since there are several varieties. Try it in fruit juice first. We take it in milk. Experiment with baked goods, casseroles, and any recipe where its taste will be neutralized.

Basic Bean Recipe

Use for white, haricot, kidney, pinto, lima, or other dry beans except soybeans. (See Basic Soybean Recipe, page 38.)

$1\frac{1}{2}$ pints water or vegetable   1 lb beans
   cooking water

Bring the water or vegetable cooking water to a full boil. Add beans slowly so that the boiling does not stop. Cover and reduce to simmer. Cook until nearly tender, about 2 hours, before adding salt or any other ingredient.

California Quiche

1 lb courgettes or chopped
   Swiss chard, or mixed
   courgettes and greens
½ onion, thinly sliced
4 eggs

6–8 oz grated cheese,
   preferably Gruyère
salt and pepper to taste
½ teaspoon each of dried
   oregano and basil

Steam courgettes and onion. Do not oversteam. Meanwhile beat the eggs and add the grated cheese. Mash courgettes (don't purée as chunks are good), and add to eggs. Add salt, pepper, oregano, and basil. Pour into greased baking dish and bake covered in 325°F, gas 3, oven until set, about 30 to 40 minutes.

Perfect as second dish at dinner.

Variation: For a one-dish meal, add fresh crab, shrimps, or any leftover cut-up chicken.

Nut Loaf

¾ lb greens (chard, spinach,
   turnip, or beet)
3 tablespoons oil
1 medium onion, sliced
   thin and chopped
2 tablespoons fresh, chopped
   parsley
1 garlic clove, mashed

1 teaspoon dried oregano
ground almonds, walnuts, or
   pecans, or in combination
3 oz dried whole-wheat
   bread crumbs
2 oz wheat germ
6 tablespoons tomato sauce
   (page 25)
1 tablespoon soy sauce

Chop and steam greens for 5 minutes. Sauté in oil the onion, parsley, garlic, and oregano. Combine all remaining in-

gredients. (Incidentally, ground nuts are better than chopped,
which tend to become too dry.) Shape into a loaf and bake at
350°F, gas 4, for 30 minutes. This loaf is not as firm as a meat
loaf, so cut gently.

Basic Soybean Recipe

6 oz dried soybeans   1 pint water

To prepare: Soak soybeans in rather less than half a pint of
the water for 1 to 2 hours; then place in flat dish in freezing
compartment overnight.

To cook: Remove from freezer; crack to remove from tray
and drop into the remaining generous half pint boiling water.
Cover. Reduce heat to simmer for 3 to 4 hours. The last hour
is the time to add onions, seasonings, oil or ham, spices,
tomatoes, or soy sauce. There are many ways to improve the
palatability of soybeans. Imagination and experimentation may
create a favourite recipe.

Super Soybean Casserole

1 slice salt pork or 2 or 3
   rashers bacon, or 2
   tablespoons of oil, topped
   in the last few minutes with
   vegetarian bacon bits
1 green pepper, diced
1 onion, chopped
1 garlic clove, mashed

scant ½ pint milk
2 teaspoons flour
2 teaspoons butter
4 oz cooked soybeans (see
   Basic Soybean Recipe,
   above)
salt and pepper to taste

Chop salt pork or bacon and brown in frying pan. Meanwhile
add vegetables to half-cooked meat and sauté together with

garlic. Then make white sauce of milk, flour, and butter. Add both mixtures to soybeans. (These should have no excess liquid after cooking. If there is, pour it into freezer jar and save for soup.) Add seasonings. Put in medium oven dish and bake at 350°F, gas 4. Serves 4 to 5.

Tofu-Egg Omelet

½ lb tofu (see page 35)	2 teaspoons salt
8 eggs, slightly beaten	1 teaspoon dried oregano
2 oz wheat germ	1 teaspoon baking powder
2 oz whole-wheat flour	2 tablespoons oil

Mix all ingredients, except the oil, well. Put oil in a large heavy frying pan and let it get quite hot over a medium heat. Pour in batter and reduce heat. Cook on the first side until fairly well set. Then turn and continue to turn occasionally until the centre is firm and can be pierced with a toothpick cleanly. This turning usually takes about 45 minutes over a low heat. Cut in pie wedges.

Use cottage cheese if tofu is not available.

Simple Mexican Pinto Beans

2 pints water	½ medium onion, sliced
1 lb pinto beans	2 tablespoons vegetable oil or
salt	½ ham hock
2 cloves garlic, mashed	

Bring water to the boil and add beans slowly, trying not to stifle the boil. Reduce heat and simmer for 30 minutes. Add salt, garlic, and onion. Simmer for another 30 minutes. Add oil or ham hock, and cook until beans are tender. Makes a good broth. Serve in bowls with warm Whole-Wheat Tortillas (see page 87).

Cottage Cheese Lunch Loaf

1 pint cottage cheese
2 spring onions, finely
   chopped

2 oz chopped walnuts
2 tablespoons soy sauce
dash of paprika

Mix all ingredients together and form a loaf on a flat serving dish. Chill for 3 hours. Serve on top of lettuce leaves.

Cottage Cheese Soufflé

4 tablespoons oil
3 oz flour
¼ pint milk
1 teaspoon each of salt and
   pepper

4 eggs, separated
1 large carton cottage cheese
2 oz Gruyère cheese, grated
1 teaspoon curry powder
juice of 1 lemon

Heat oil in 1-quart saucepan. Add flour and stir constantly while adding milk gradually. Cook until a thick sauce. Remove from heat. Add salt and pepper, well-beaten egg yolks, cottage cheese, grated cheese, curry, and lemon juice. Fold in stiffly beaten egg whites. Pour into a 2½ pint baking dish. Bake 1 hour at 300°F, gas 2. Serve immediately. Serves 3 to 4.

Macaroni, Egg, and Cheese

2½ pints salted water
8 oz soy, wheat, or sesame
  macaroni
8 oz Cheddar cheese
3 eggs, well beaten with 2
  tablespoons milk or cream

salt and pepper
4 tablespoons whole-wheat
  bread crumbs
2 tablespoons wheat germ

Bring water to the boil. Add macaroni slowly, reduce heat, and cook until tender. Strain. Add cheese, eggs, and salt and pepper to taste. Pour in oiled 3-pint casserole. Bake covered for 20 minutes at 325°F, gas 3 (or until eggs are set). Mix together bread crumbs and wheat germ and sprinkle over casserole; set casserole under grill 3 inches from heat source until a golden crust forms. Serves 3 to 4.

Lentil-Mushroom Stew

2½ pints stock or water
1 lb lentils, washed
1 onion, sliced and chopped
½ lb mushrooms, sliced
1 teaspoon dried basil
½ teaspoon salt
2 stalks celery and tops,
  chopped

2 carrots, sliced
1 medium-sized can
  tomatoes
4 tablespoons oil
2 tablespoons vinegar

Bring stock to the boil and slowly add lentils. Reduce to a simmer and cook 1 hour. Meanwhile sauté onion, mushrooms, and basil in oil. Set aside. Combine all ingredients, except vinegar and seasonings, and cook at least 1 more hour, or until lentils are tender. Add vinegar before serving. Add salt and pepper to taste. Serves 4 well.

This can be served over Simple Brown Rice (see page 69).

Split Pea-Vegetable Stew

2½ pints stock	2 potatoes, peeled and cubed
1 lb split peas	1 bay leaf
3 oz barley	1 clove garlic, minced
3 stalks celery, chopped	4 tablespoons oil
1 onion, sliced and chopped	½ teaspoon salt
greens, chopped, are good (optional)	2 teaspoons caraway seeds

Bring stock to the boil and slowly add split peas and barley. Reduce to simmer and cook 1 hour. Meanwhile sauté vegetables, bay leaf, and garlic in the oil. Combine with stew, add salt, and cook about 1 more hour. Add caraway seeds and simmer 30 minutes longer. Serves 4.

Yogurt

4 oz of non-instant powdered milk	1¼ pints warm water, or enough to fill blender after other ingredients added
2 tablespoons fresh yogurt (preferably from a natural food store)	

Blend all the ingredients well, pour in quart, screw-top glass jars, and place in an electric incubator. Incubation time varies from 4 to 6 hours. The yogurt is done when it can be separated with a knife, as with custard.

For a home-made incubator, use a box and an electric heating pad, or place the jars in a pan of warm water in an oven that is kept warm by the pilot light. Home-made incubation is not always successful.

To use pasteurized or homogenized milk, you must first heat the milk to just below boiling. Cool to lukewarm before adding the starter.

Yogurt is commonly served with fruit. We would like to suggest topping your serving of yogurt with 1 or 2 teaspoons of raw wheat germ and 2 or 3 tablespoons of honey, or more if you favour it sweeter.

Meat,
Fowl, and
Fish

In spite of the move towards vegetarian diets, meat consumption is at an all-time high in this country and shows no immediate sign of decreasing. Given this fact, and our own feeling that a healthy diet should contain some meat, fowl, and fish, we have included a variety of recipes in this area. At the same time, we are obliged to express our concern and dissatisfaction with the inferior conditions under which these animals have been raised (see the Introduction).

When cooking meat, fish, or fowl, it is best to use a low temperature which allows the connecting tissues to break down evenly as the heat penetrates. Juices are lost as the meat becomes hotter. At temperatures above 170°F, protein begins to get tough and dry. Another way to avoid drying meat is to add salt in the last part of the cooking period. Salt draws out the juices and should be used only when this is desired, as for stew or soups. Coat very lean meat and chicken with oil before roasting to hold in the juices.

One man to know is your butcher. Become acquainted with him. Ask him questions about his meat and make him feel like an authority, which in many ways he is. Don't hesitate to select exactly the piece you want. Look it over carefully before you buy it. When, after careful preparation, it doesn't meet your expectations, tell him. If you are always as certain to tell him when the meat is good, you will have a friend.

Potato-Prune Roast

1¾ lb of chuck roast
juice of 1 lemon
3 tablespoons natural sugar
1 lb prunes

2 or 3 potatoes, peeled and
chopped (1 to 2 inches)
3 or 4 carrots, chopped same
size as potatoes

Trim some of the fat from the meat. Melt it in a pan and brown
the meat slowly. Then add enough water to cover five-eighths
of the meat. Add lemon, sugar, and prunes. Reduce heat and
simmer 2 to 3 hours, depending on thickness of meat. Remove
meat, put vegetables in pot, place meat on top, cover, and put
in 325°F, gas 3, oven for one more hour, or until vegetables
are tender.

This is a dish that needs an ample amount of juice, so watch
to see that it does not get dry. Wonderful the next day.
Serves 4.

Norwegian Meatballs

¼ pint milk
4 oz bread crumbs
3 teaspoons finely minced
onion
2 tablespoons oil
2 lb minced beef

1 egg
salt and pepper
¼ teaspoon nutmeg
1 can consommé, or ½ pint
beef stock

Soak the crumbs in the milk. Sauté onion in oil. Remove from
pan and mix together all the ingredients, except the consommé. Shape into small balls, about 1 inch in diameter.
Brown well on all sides in hot oil. Heat consommé in deep pot
and, as meatballs finish browning, place them in the hot

consommé. Simmer for approximately 30 minutes over low heat.

Sweet and Sour Stew

1 lb stewing beef	½ lb mushrooms, sliced
3 tablespoons oil	4 tablespoons tomato sauce
¾ pint water	(see page 25)
1 onion, sliced	3 tablespoons red-wine
salt and pepper	vinegar
4 carrots, chopped in 1-inch	2 oz natural sugar
pieces	1 tablespoon Worcester sauce

Trim meat and cut into 1-inch pieces. Brown well in hot oil. Reduce heat and add half the water. Add onion, salt, and pepper. Simmer 1½ hours. Add carrots and mushrooms. Combine tomato sauce, vinegar, sugar, Worcester sauce, and remaining water and add to meat. Simmer together for 1 more hour, or until meat is tender. Serve over soy or wheat noodles (homemade pasta is nice). Serves 4 to 6.

Skewered Veal

2 lb lean veal, cut in 1-inch	4 tablespoons soy sauce
squares	4 tablespoons lemon juice
1 lb large, fresh mushrooms,	4 tablespoons oil
washed	1 clove garlic, mashed

Skewer veal alternately with mushrooms. Mix soy sauce, lemon, oil, and garlic. Marinate meat in this mixture for 4 to 6 hours. Grill for 10 to 12 minutes, or over charcoal for 15 to 20 minutes, until golden. Baste while grilling. Serve with Barley-Mushroom Pilaf (see page 70).

Stuffed Cabbage

1 very large cabbage

Sauce :
1 onion, sliced thin
3 tablespoons oil
1 medium can tomatoes
½ teaspoon paprika
½ teaspoon dill
salt and pepper
juice of 1 lemon

Stuffing :
½ lb pork sausagemeat
1 clove garlic, mashed
salt and pepper
4 oz cooked rice
2 eggs
1 teaspoon paprika
½ teaspoon thyme

Remove 12 to 14 whole cabbage leaves carefully, and steam on rack above ½ pint of water until leaves are tender and bend without tearing.

Prepare sauce by sautéing the onion in oil. Add the rest of the sauce ingredients, the water from the cabbage leaves, and the remaining part of the cabbage, sliced thin. Simmer for 20 to 30 minutes.

Brown the sausagemeat and garlic with salt and pepper. Mix with rice, eggs, paprika, and thyme.

Spoon 1 or 2 tablespoons stuffing into the centre of each cabbage leaf and roll up tightly. Place carefully in a deep pan and cover with sauce. Cover and simmer for 45 minutes to 1 hour. Serves 5 to 6.

Beef Stew

2 to 3 lb chuck steak
whole-wheat flour
1 pint water
2 tablespoons tomato paste
salt and pepper
1 clove garlic

1 bay leaf
4 medium carrots, sliced
1 medium onion, quartered
1 large potato, cut in pieces
1 large turnip, cut in pieces

Cut steak into stew-sized pieces. Trim fat. Dredge in 2 oz flour
and brown in a heavy stew pan over moderate heat. Add water,
tomato paste, salt and pepper, garlic, and bay leaf. Simmer 1
hour. Add onion and carrots and simmer for another hour, or
until tender. The potato and turnip are put in for the last
20 minutes. Add more flour for desired thickness. Serves 6.

Sauerbraten

1½ pints cider vinegar	6 bay leaves
1½ pints water	6 peppercorns
3 onions, sliced thin	3 tablespoons salt
1 lemon, sliced thin	6 lb rump beef
12 whole cloves	3 tablespoons oil

To prepare: Make a marinade by mixing all the ingredients,
except the meat and oil, in a large bowl. Add the meat; turn
once or twice and cover. Refrigerate for 24 to 28 hours. Turn
meat in marinade occasionally.

To cook: Use a heavy, deep pan. Remove meat and shake
off marinade. Brown well in hot oil over medium heat. Add
¾ pint of strained marinade and simmer, covered, for 4 to 5
hours. Remove meat and thicken juice with enough flour to
make a gravy. Slice meat and serve with noodles and gravy.
Serves 8 to 10.

Marinated Beef Tongue

1 beef tongue, 2 or 3 lb	1 clove garlic, mashed
¾ pint vegetable stock	2 oz sliced mushrooms
6 tablespoons oil	2 tablespoons oil
6 tablespoons lemon juice	6 tablespoons tomato juice or
½ onion, sliced thin	sauce (see page 25)
1 teaspoon fresh, finely	salt and pepper to taste
chopped parsley	1 teaspoon sherry

To cook tongue: Scrub tongue with a brush and place on a rack above ¾ pint of vegetable stock. Steam gently for 2 to 3 hours, or until tender. Remove while hot and trim gristle at the base of the tongue. Remove the entire skin. (It is easier to remove the skin while hot.) Slice diagonally at the tip and parallel at the base from the outside toward the middle.

Mix half the oil with the lemon juice and marinate the slices of meat for one hour. Sauté onion, parsley, garlic, and mushrooms in remaining oil. Add tomato juice. Add tongue, lemon marinade, and seasoning and simmer together for 12 to 15 minutes. Add sherry just before serving. Serve tongue and sauce in large soup bowls with noodles. Serves 5 to 6.

Lamb Loaf

1 large onion, chopped	1 lb minced lamb
1 oz fresh parsley, minced	½ teaspoon salt
1 clove garlic, mashed	½ teaspoon dried dill
1 tablespoon oil	pepper
1 egg	1 slice bread, soaked in water
1 oz wheat germ	and squeezed dry

Sauté onion, parsley, and garlic in oil. Mix all ingredients together and shape into a loaf. Bake at 325°F, gas 3, for 1 hour. Serves 4 to 5.

Note: Beef may be used instead of lamb.

Sweetbreads Italian

1 lb sweetbreads	3 tablespoons butter
1½ pints water	1 teaspoon dried oregano
1 tablespoon vinegar	6 tablespoons Madeira
1 lb mushrooms, sliced	2 tablespoons Worcester
2 oz fresh parsley, chopped	sauce
1 clove garlic, minced	salt and pepper

To prepare: Soak sweetbreads for 30 minutes in cold water to cover. Change water once. Drain and place in saucepan. Add 1½ pints of cold water and 1 tablespoon vinegar and bring slowly to the boil. Reduce heat and simmer for 5 minutes. Drain well and break into sections. Remove excess cartilage and tissues, but leave fragile membrane around smaller sections.

To cook: Sauté mushrooms and parsley and garlic in butter for 4 to 5 minutes. Add sweetbreads and sauté another 4 to 5 minutes. Add oregano and liquids and simmer gently 10 to 15 minutes. Salt and pepper to taste. Serve over or alongside a grain dish (see pages 68–71).

Note: Watch simmering time and do not overcook.

London Lamb Kidneys

6 lamb kidneys, with	1 oz parsley, minced
surrounding fat left on (if	salt and pepper
possible)	lemon wedges
¾ teaspoon thyme	

Wipe kidneys, do not wash. Slice, but not too thin so they will not cook too rapidly. In a heavy skillet, sauté the kidneys in their own fat if possible, with thyme, until just slightly pink inside. Sprinkle with parsley and serve immediately, with lemon wedges.

Note: If kidneys are without fat, use 2 tablespoons of oil and 2 tablespoons of butter.

Beef Heart with Bulgur Wheat Stuffing

1 beef heart, 4 to 5 lb	1 medium onion, chopped
1 clove garlic	1 medium carrot, chopped
2 teaspoons pepper	2 stalks celery, chopped
3 tablespoons oil	1 tablespoon fresh parsley,
2 pints vegetable stock or	chopped
bouillon	½ teaspoon dried thyme
2 rashers bacon (optional)	½ teaspoon dried rosemary
¾ lb bulgur wheat	whole-wheat flour
½ teaspoon salt	

Trim heart of fat and remove inside connective membranes. Wipe with damp cloth. Rub both sides with garlic, pepper, and 1 tablespoon oil. Place on a rack in a deep pan over ¾ pint vegetable stock. Place the rashers of bacon over heart and steam gently until tender, about 2 to 3 hours. Do not overcook.

To prepare stuffing: Bring 1¼ pints vegetable stock or water to the boil. Add the bulgur wheat and salt. Reduce heat and simmer 15 to 20 minutes. Meanwhile, sauté onion, celery, and carrot in remaining oil for approximately 4 to 5 minutes. Mix with seasonings and cooked bulgur wheat.

Place stuffing on bottom of a baking dish. Remove heart and place on the stuffing. Cover with foil. Bake in preheated 350°F, gas 4, oven for 20 to 30 minutes. Retain broth from heart and thicken with enough whole-wheat flour for gravy. Slice heart thin for serving and pour the gravy over the meat. Serves 6.

After steaming, heart can also be minced for a meat loaf; or it can be sliced thin, breaded, and fried quickly in vegetable oil.

African Chicken with Hot Greens

1 medium frying chicken, cut up	½ pint water, boiling
1 lb mustard greens or spinach	2 chicken bouillon cubes
1 large onion	10 small, red, dried chili peppers

Brown chicken well in its own fat. Use heavy, deep pan and brown slowly. Meanwhile cut up greens coarsely. Slice onion fine.

Make a broth of water, bouillon cubes, diced heart and liver of chicken, and peppers. Crush the peppers between fingers, being certain to wash hands well afterward to avoid smarting. Simmer.

When chicken is well browned, pour a quarter of the sauce over chicken and reduce heat. Lay ¾ sliced onion over chicken, then the greens over the onion, followed by the remaining onion. Pour remaining sauce over all. Cover and steam until done, about 1½ hours, without stirring. Serve with a grain (see pages 68–71). Serves 4 to 6.

Liver Sautéed in Wheat Germ

6 tablespoons oil	salt and pepper to taste
1 large onion, sliced thin	1 lb calf's liver, sliced thin
4 oz wheat germ	
1 oz grated Parmesan cheese (optional)	

Heat 3 tablespoons oil in heavy skillet and sauté onion until clear. Remove and set aside. Mix wheat germ, Parmesan, salt and pepper. Heat remaining oil in pan. Dredge liver in wheat germ mixture and sauté over low heat until cooked through. Serves 4 to 5.

Sweet and Sour Chicken

1 medium frying chicken, cut up
6 tablespoons wine vinegar
6 tablespoons soy sauce
2 garlic cloves, mashed
salt and pepper

1 teaspoon prepared mustard
¼ pint tomato sauce (see page 25)
4 tablespoons honey or
2 oz natural sugar

Wash and dry the chicken. Put in 3-pint casserole and cover with sauce made of remaining ingredients. Cover and bake at 325°F, gas 3, for 2 hours, or until very tender. Turn frequently while baking. Serves 4 to 5.

Grecian Chicken

1 medium frying chicken, cut up
2 tablespoons oil
salt and pepper

¾ pint tomato sauce (see page 25)
2 oz black olives, sliced
2 teaspoons cinnamon

Wash and dry the chicken. Brown well in oil in a heavy pan. Salt and pepper to taste. Mix tomato sauce, olives, and cinnamon. Combine chicken and sauce in a covered oven dish. Bake at 325°F, gas 3, for 1½ to 2 hours, turning occasionally. Chicken is done when meat falls away from the bone. Serves 4 to 5.

Chicken Cacciatore

1 (3-lb) chicken, cut up	salt and pepper to taste
3 tablespoons oil	1 green pepper, cut up
½ medium onion	6 large mushrooms, sliced
2 cloves garlic	¼ pint tomato sauce (see
1 oz fresh, chopped parsley	page 25)
2 oz butter, melted	¼ pint water

Fry chicken in hot oil until brown. Do not cook through. Arrange chicken in baking dish. Chop onion, garlic, and parsley until fine, add to melted butter, and sauté lightly. Pour over chicken. Add salt and pepper. Add pepper and mushrooms to top of chicken. Pour tomato sauce and water over top and bake 1 hour at 350°F, gas 4.

Sesame Fish

2 lb fish fillets, sole, halibut, cod, haddock or other	6 tablespoons breadcrumbs
salt and pepper	4 tablespoons sesame seeds
1 egg	4 tablespoons oil
2 tablespoons milk	1 oz fresh parsley, chopped
2 oz flour	3 tablespoons lemon juice
	1 small onion, chopped fine

Season fish with salt and pepper. Beat egg and milk together. Dip each fillet lightly into flour, then into liquid, then into breadcrumbs and seeds mixed together.

Heat oil hot, reduce heat, and fry 3 to 8 minutes, depending on thickness of fish. Absorb excess oil by draining on paper towels. Combine parsley, lemon juice, and onion and pour over fish before serving. Serves 5 to 6.

Squid Adriatic

1 large onion, thinly sliced
2 large cloves garlic, mashed
4 tablespoons olive oil
2–3 oz fresh parsley, chopped
1 medium green pepper, sliced thin
1 teaspoon fresh, chopped tarragon, or ⅓ teaspoon dried

1 teaspoon dried oregano
1 large tin tomatoes, coarsely chopped. If fresh are used, add about ½ pint water
1 teaspoon salt
¾ lb sliced mushrooms
3 or 4 lb cleaned squid
¾ pint water

Sauté onion and 1 clove garlic slightly in 2 tablespoons oil. Add parsley and pepper and sauté 3 to 5 more minutes, retaining 2 tablespoons of parsley for the squid. Add rest of the sauce ingredients and simmer 1½ hours.

To cook squid: Squid should be cooked separately as it has a lot of water which can cause the broth to be too fishy. Do not cut up squid. Steam above ¾ pint of water for 15 minutes, or until it turns pink. Overcooking will cause squid to become tough. While steaming, pour over it a mixture of 2 tablespoons oil, 2 tablespoons parsley, and 1 clove garlic, mashed.

Put steamed squid in the hot sauce and serve immediately in flat soup bowls alongside Polenta (see page 71). Make double recipe of Polenta. Serves 8.

Barley-stuffed Squid

12 (1½ lb) squid bodies, still in tube form
1 medium onion, chopped
1 oz fresh parsley, chopped
5–6 oz mushrooms, chopped
2 cloves garlic, mashed

3 tablespoons oil
tentacles, chopped small
6–8 oz cooked barley
1 teaspoon dried basil
6 tablespoons white wine

Steam squid bodies as directed in recipe for Squid Adriatic (see page 58). Sauté onion, parsley, mushrooms, and garlic in oil. Add tentacles 3 to 4 minutes later and sauté 3 to 4 more minutes.

Mix barley with sautéed vegetables and basil. Stuff bodies and place side by side in a flat oven dish. Cover with wine and foil. Bake at 350°F, gas 4, for 15 to 20 minutes. Serves 4 to 5.

Plaice in Egg Batter

1 lb plaice or flounder	1 teaspoon dried dill
2 eggs	1 clove mashed garlic
½ teaspoon dried oregano	pinch of cayenne
¼ teaspoon cumin	4 tablespoons oil
salt and pepper	lemon wedges

Fillet the fish. Beat together all the remaining ingredients, except the oil and lemon, to make batter. Heat oil in heavy skillet. Dip fish in batter and fry 5 to 6 minutes on one side. Turn and fry until flaky. During the last few minutes, pour remaining batter over the fish and cook without stirring, as for an omelet. Serve with lemon wedges. Serves 4.

Curried Oysters and Corn

1 lb oysters	2 eggs, slightly beaten
2 tablespoons oil	1¼ teaspoons curry powder
2 tablespoons butter	6 tablespoons bread crumbs
1 small onion, chopped	2 oz grated cheese
1 large can creamed corn	

Cut oysters in bite-size pieces. Heat oil and butter and sauté onion and oysters briefly, about 4 to 5 minutes. Remove and boil down remaining liquid. Add corn. Place in small, greased casserole. Stir in beaten eggs, curry powder, oysters, and onions. Cover with crumbs and bake for 20 to 25 minutes at 350°F, gas 4. Sprinkle on cheese the last few minutes. Serves 4.

Grain Dishes

Learning about grains is fun for most people who are interested in cooking as well as baking. Once you have a knowledge of the variety of available grains, you will enjoy browsing in natural food stores. A few grain forms are sold in some supermarkets – bulgur wheat (ala), kasha (buckwheat groats), rolled oats, barley, and, increasingly, natural brown rice. Learn to use grains as substitutes for potatoes, white-flour pastas, and white rice.

WHOLE WHEAT. Whole-wheat grains, or wheat berries, are a wonderful accompaniment to meat, fish, and fowl. They can also be prepared as a pilaf with vegetables as a main dish. The texture is chewy. Whole wheat is a good source of B vitamins and minerals.

BULGUR WHEAT. Bulgur wheat is wheat which has been prepared for cooking by cracking, steaming, and toasting. It is valuable because of its high nutritional content in relation to its short preparational period. Bulgur wheat may sometimes be found in shops under the name *ala*.

OATS. Old-fashioned rolled oats require very little cooking to be palatable and are a good hearty breakfast for children, especially when sprinkled with a little wheat germ. Natural-food stores and grain supply houses offer oat groats, unhulled oats, and steel-cut oats. They can be used for more textured cereals, as well as additions to breads, cookies, and muffins. Steamed oat flakes are sold in supermarkets as quick-cooking oats. They have slightly less nutritional value.

RYE. Rye is a staple grain in northern Europe and Russia. It is hardy and can be grown in any soil. Many nutritionists think it tends to create stronger muscles than wheat. It can be bought in the whole grain for home grinding, or in grits to use as a cereal or in breads.

CORN. Corn is native to the Americas and a staple of Mexico and some South American countries. It is a good source of inositol, a B vitamin. Do avoid refined commercial cornmeal, which contains little nutritional value and has been prepared from sterile hybrid corn. Instead buy coarse ground cornmeal from natural food stores. It is also sold whole for home grinding and popping.

RICE. Most rice consumed today has been processed like wheat, with the outer husk and germ removed, leaving only starch. Natural brown rice is preferable in nutrition and tastes better. The 'converted' rice on sale in some places is said to have been processed in a manner which forces the vitamins into the centre of the rice, thus saving them from being lost in the chaff during milling. Rice polish and rice bran are the outer layers of the rice when natural rice is converted to white. The polishings, especially, are nice additions to baked goods and cereals.

BARLEY. Barley is another Eastern European grain. The pearl barley found in markets today is mostly starch, so we recommend buying the hulled or unhulled variety from mills or natural food stores. Barley grits are also available. Barley is a good addition to soups and casseroles, and makes a tasty rice substitute.

BUCKWHEAT. Buckwheat is a plant whose seeds are hulled and cracked for quick preparation. Sometimes sold under the term *groats* or the Russian name *kasha*, it has a very different, hearty taste and is a good source of B vitamins. Use it as a side dish for meats and in casseroles. It is excellent with pot roast and gravy.

MILLET. This grain is a staple in many African countries and a favourite of the legendary Hunzas. A good source of protein, calcium, and lecithin, it cooks fast and is easily digestible. Use millet as a side dish, a cereal, a pudding, or in soup or bread. It also comes in meal form.

WHEAT GERM. In the centre of the wheat kernel is the embryo, or germ, of the wheat which contains most of the vitamins and minerals. Extracted and sold separately, the germ is especially rich in vitamin E, but, because of its high oil content, it must be kept refrigerated to prevent rancidity. Use it on yogurt, on cereals, in baked goods and casseroles, and for breading.

Many nutritious cereal preparations are found in natural food stores, and they are beginning to appear in supermarkets.

Familia

10 oz quick oats
6 oz raw or toasted wheat
  germ
½ lb dried apricots, cut up
4–5 oz chopped nuts

10 oz rolled wheat or wheat
  flakes
10 oz raisins
4 oz natural sugar (optional)

Mix everything together and store in jars in the refrigerator.

You may substitute or add any dried fruits or nuts available. Any flaked grain may be used, such as bran, rye, etc. Familia is eaten raw with milk and honey.

Crunchy Dry Cereal

10 oz rolled oats
4 oz wheat germ
4 oz sesame seeds
4 oz shredded, unsweetened
  coconut

3 tablespoons oil
9 tablespoons honey
1 teaspoon vanilla
dash of salt

Mix all ingredients. Spread ½ inch deep on a baking sheet. Bake at 250°F, gas 1, until golden brown. Stir occasionally, as sides brown first. Let cool. Store in jars. Serve with milk.

Seven-grain Dry Cereal

10 oz rolled bran
10 oz millet flour
10 oz oatmeal
10 oz cornmeal
6 oz whole-wheat flour
4 oz wheat germ

1 oz soy grits
1 tablespoon salt
1½ pints milk or soy milk
4 oz dry malt
4 tablespoons honey

Blend all ingredients together except milk, malt, and honey. Mix these separately, and add to the rest to make a stiff dough. Roll out very thin. Prick with a fork and place on a greased baking sheet. Bake at 300°F, gas 2, until golden brown. Cool and put through a food chopper or crumble with hands.

Cream of Rice

1 teaspoon oil   2 cups water
1 cup brown rice   1 teaspoon salt

To prepare: Heat the oil in a heavy pan. Sauté rice until golden brown. The oil is only to prevent sticking. Put rice into a blender and grind into a meal at high speed. Store in the refrigerator or use immediately. You can make a much larger quantity for future use (add a little more water if needed).

To cook: Bring 2 cups of water to the boil. Add rice and salt. Reduce heat to low and simmer until desired thickness is reached, approximately 30 minutes. Stir frequently.

Millet Porridge

½ cup millet   ¾ teaspoon salt
1 cup water

Soak millet overnight in water. Bring to the boil in the morning, add salt, and cook, covered, for 20 minutes in the top of a double boiler. Mixture will be thick and can be thinned with water or hot milk if desired. Serve with honey and milk. Serves 3 to 4.

Oat Porridge

½ cup oats   ½ teaspoon salt
2½ cups water

Pour oats slowly into boiling salted water. Cover and simmer

30 minutes. Add more water if necessary for desired consistency. Serve with honey and milk.

Cornmeal Mush

1 cup cornmeal   2 teaspoons salt
3½ or 4 cups milk or water,
   or mixture of both

Combine meal with 1 cup cold liquid. When smooth, add the rest of the liquid (either boiling water or scalded milk). Add salt and cook 30 minutes in the top of a double boiler, stirring occasionally. Milk makes the most nourishing porridge for children. Serve with honey and milk.

Kasha (Buckwheat)

1 cup buckwheat   2 cups boiling water
1 egg, slightly beaten   ½ teaspoon salt

Put buckwheat and egg in a skillet. Stir constantly over a high heat. After each grain is separate and dry, add boiling water and salt, and reduce heat. Cover tightly and steam for 30 minutes. Serve with butter and salt to taste. Serves 3 to 4.

Bulgur Wheat

1 cup bulgur wheat   2 cups stock or water
1 teaspoon oil

Sauté bulgur in oil until the grains are slightly browned. Reduce heat and add stock slowly. Cover and simmer for 15 minutes, or until grain has absorbed the liquid. You can add any vegetables to make a pilaf.

Whole Wheat

6 cups water or consommé   2 teaspoons salt
2 cups whole wheat

Bring liquid to the boil. Add wheat slowly. Reduce heat and simmer very gently 3 to 4 hours, or until wheat is tender. Watch the liquid. Add salt the last hour. Serve with butter or soy sauce. It will be chewier than rice.

Simple Brown Rice

4 cups water   1 teaspoon salt
2 cups rice

Bring water to the boil. Add rice slowly. Reduce heat and add salt. Simmer for 1 hour, or until tender. Serve with butter or soy sauce.

Brown Rice Baked in Consommé

1 medium onion, chopped   4 tablespoons oil
2 tablespoons fresh parsley,   2 cups brown rice
  chopped   4 cups consommé or bouillon

Sauté onion and parsley in the oil in a heavy frying pan. Add rice and sauté again lightly. Remove from heat and add broth. Pour into a 3-pint casserole and bake at 325°F, gas 3, for 1 hour, or until tender. Serves 4 to 6.

Brown Rice Burgers

8 oz cooked brown rice
2 oz parsley, chopped
3 raw carrots, grated
1 large onion, chopped
1 clove garlic, mashed

salt and pepper
1 egg
2 oz whole-wheat flour
3 to 4 tablespoons oil

Mix together all ingredients except oil until well blended. Add more flour if mixture is too soft to form patties. Put oil on hands and form patties. Fry in oil.

Can be served hot or cold. They keep well in refrigerator and make a good substitute for sandwiches in school lunches.

Barley-Mushroom Pilaf

½ lb mushrooms, diced
1 tablespoon fresh, finely
   chopped parsley
1 small onion, diced
1 lb barley

6 tablespoons oil
1½ pints chicken broth
salt and pepper
1 bay leaf

Sauté mushrooms, parsley, onion, and barley in oil. Put into a 3-pint casserole with broth and seasonings, and cover. Bake at 350°F, gas 4, for 45 minutes, or until barley is tender and liquid is absorbed. Serves 4 to 6.

Millet Hunza Style

Cook millet according to directions for Millet Porridge (see page 67). Chop an onion finely, sauté it and mix with the millet and/or top with grated cheese. Serves 3 to 4.

Millet Soufflé

4 oz cooked millet
½ teaspoon salt
pepper
3 egg yolks, beaten

¼ pint milk
2 oz grated cheese
3 egg whites, stiffly beaten

Mix all ingredients together, reserving 1 oz cheese for the top and folding in stiffly beaten egg whites last. Pour in greased baking dish and top with grated cheese. Put the dish in a pan of hot water and bake in moderate oven until it sets, approximately 20 minutes. Serves 4 to 5.

Polenta

For use with a meat or fish soup or stew.

4 oz cornmeal
scant ½ pint water
1 teaspoon salt
1 teaspoon paprika

dash of cayenne
3 oz grated cheese
5–6 tablespoons meat or fish
   sauce

In the top of a double boiler combine cornmeal, water, and salt, adding the cornmeal very slowly to avoid lumping. Mix well, add paprika and cayenne, and steam over low heat for 30 minutes. Turn into an oiled baking dish or casserole and bake at 350°F, gas 4, for 10 to 15 minutes. Top with grated cheese and/or a few tablespoons of sauce from the meat or fish dish. Put under the grill until a brown crust is formed. Serves 4.

Variation: Drop by spoonfuls into a broth or soup.

Whole-Wheat Pasta

3 eggs
1 lb sifted whole-wheat flour

1½ teaspoons salt
3–6 tablespoons water

To prepare: Beat eggs well. Sift flour into a heap on a large, clear surface, and make a well in the middle. Put eggs and salt in the well and mix, adding water a little at a time to keep the dough soft for working. Keep sprinkling flour on to the egg, mixing all the time until the eggs and flour are well mixed. Transfer to a floured board and knead well for 10 minutes. When the dough is light and elastic, divide into three to four parts. Roll out each part very thin into a rectangle and then roll them up like Swiss rolls. Leave to dry for 30 minutes. Cut into thin strips.

To cook: Use a large pan nearly full of boiling, well-salted water. Add pasta and continue to boil until the pasta is done to your taste. You can add a little oil to the water to prevent sticking.

Breads and
Quick Breads

All the grains discussed in the last chapter are ground into flours and meals for baking and breading, and broken into grits for adding to casseroles and cereals. Many flour and meal labels say 'stone-ground', which indicates that the milling was done on a soft buhrstone, an age-old process which involves a slow grinding of the entire grain. After the industrial revolution, for expedience and volume, this method was almost totally replaced by fast roller mills in which the vital germ – containing 90 per cent of the nutrients – was discarded because it became rancid from the heat of these high-speed mills and tended to stick in the machinery. Along with the extraction of the germ, chemical bleaches were added to make the flour whiter. For years, the public has been deluded into thinking this flour is somehow 'nicer' than the heavier whole-grain flours.

In the last fifty years, however, many milling machines have been developed which equal the output of the roller mills without extracting the germ from the flour. These new machines spread the germ evenly throughout the flour. What we want to stress is that there is no argument left for refined flours. When the ground germ is spread evenly in the flour, the problem of rancidity is not a real danger if the flour is packaged tightly and not allowed to sit in humid areas. It is best to refrigerate whole-grain flours, especially whole wheat, after opening the package, if you need to store the flour for any length of time. It is wise to watch for flours which are milled near by and to patronize natural food stores and markets where there is a good turnover in flour. You can also freeze flour if you wish to purchase it in large quantities.

Before experimenting with too many flours and grains, we suggest you learn the basics of baking. The lightness of bread depends not only on the leavening, but also on the level of gluten or wheat protein in the flour. When flour is kneaded or stirred, the gluten forces the flour to stick together in thin elastic sheets and catch the gas from the yeast. This process makes the bread rise. Wheat flour contains the most gluten and rye flour has some gluten, but all other flours lack this element and tend to neutralize its effect. The germ of the wheat grain has no gluten; therefore, you should add the non-wheat flours and chaffs last, after the yeast has had a chance to work with the gluten.

When making your own bread, it is wise to make a sponge first. Dissolve the yeast in lukewarm liquid and then add all the liquid required in the recipe, the sweetener, and about $\frac{1}{2}$ to $\frac{3}{4}$ lb of the flour containing gluten. It should be the consistency of pancake batter. Mix well, cover with a damp cloth, and set in a warm place. Let it rise for 1 hour. Stir again and add the remaining ingredients. Then cover and allow the dough to rise double. A sponge encourages quick rising and is especially effective with heavy flours.

We strongly suggest using gluten flour in bread that calls for soy flour, since soy flour is heavy and needs the effect of gluten. Gluten flour is produced by a process which washes the gluten out of the whole-wheat flour. The remainder, or gluten, is dried and ground into flour. It is sold in natural food stores and mills.

It is a good idea to add powdered milk to your baked goods for extra protein. When substituting honey or molasses for sugar in your own recipes, reduce by one third the amount called for.

When making quick breads, it is important to understand the leavening agents. Baking soda is considered to destroy B vitamins in whole-wheat flour and should be avoided. We have substituted baking powder for soda in our recipes, although there is a little bicarbonate of soda in all baking powders. When choosing a brand of baking powder, do not buy those which contain aluminium compounds.

If you wish to avoid baking powder entirely, we suggest adding to your batter 1 or 2 tablespoons of baker's yeast dissolved in lukewarm liquid. (We feel cake yeast works faster, but dry yeast which has the moisture removed is effective and does not have to be refrigerated.) Then set the batter in a warm place for 30 to 45 minutes before baking. Stiffly beaten egg whites folded in just before baking will help add lightness. Nutritional yeast also helps baked foods to rise well.

YEAST BREADS

After dough is well mixed, transfer to a board for kneading. (While kneading, keep your hands and the board covered with flour.) Fold dough, like an omelet, toward you and then push away with the heels of your palms. Continue this process until the dough becomes smooth and elastic. Then place dough in a well-oiled bowl, turn over once, cover, and leave to rise until double. Punch raised dough down, knead again, and shape into loaves. Bread pans should always be well greased; dough should touch each edge of a loaf pan to help support it as it rises.

The oven should be preheated at least 5 minutes for bread and pastry baking. Bread is done when it is golden brown. Remove the pans from the oven and turn them on their sides. After a few minutes, remove the bread from the pans and transfer the loaves to a wire rack to cool. Bread gets damp when left in pans.

High Protein Bread

1¼ pints warm water
½ oz dry yeast
2 tablespoons honey
12 oz whole-wheat flour
1 lb unbleached flour

3 tablespoons wheat germ
2 oz soy flour or powder
3 oz skim-milk powder
4 teaspoons salt
2 tablespoons oil or butter

Combine the water, yeast, and honey. Leave to stand for 5 minutes. Measure and sift the whole-wheat and unbleached flour, wheat germ, soy flour, and skim-milk powder. Stir the yeast mixture and, while stirring, add the salt and 3 cups of the flour mixture. Beat 75 strokes or 2 minutes with an electric mixer. Add the oil and 3 cups flour mixture. Blend and then turn out on a floured board, adding 1 cup or more additional flour as needed. Knead thoroughly, about 5 minutes, until dough is smooth and elastic. Place in a well-oiled bowl and let rise until double. Punch dough down, fold over the edges, and turn dough upside down. Let it rise another 20 minutes.

Turn out on a board, shape in 2 loaves, placed in buttered bread pan, cover, and let rise until double. Bake at 350°F, gas 4, for 50 to 60 minutes. If loaves begin to brown too soon, or as soon as 15 to 20 minutes, reduce heat to 325°F, gas 3.

This recipe makes excellent rolls.

Cracked Wheat Bread

1 pint water
½ lb cracked wheat
4 tablespoons honey
1 teaspoon salt
2 tablespoons oil

½ oz dry yeast
10 oz gluten and/or
   unbleached flour
12 oz whole-wheat flour

Pour ¾ pint boiling water over the cracked wheat. Add the honey (reserving 1 teaspoon for later), salt and oil. Cool. Dissolve the yeast in ¼ pint warm water and add the 1 teaspoon honey. Combine with the cooled cracked-wheat mixture. Add the flour and mix thoroughly. Place in a buttered bowl and cover, and let rise for 1 hour. Punch down and let rise for another 30 minutes.

Punch down and turn out on a floured board. Knead well. Shape into 2 loaves and place in buttered loaf pans. Bake at 350°F, gas 4, until golden brown, about 45 or 50 minutes.

Oatmeal Bread

¼ oz dry yeast
3 tablespoons lukewarm water
1½ pints milk, boiling
6 oz rolled oats
6 tablespoons oil

6 tablespoons molasses
1 tablespoon salt
1¼ lb gluten and/or
    unbleached flour
1¾ lb whole-wheat flour

Dissolve the yeast in the warm water. Add the milk to the oats and oil and leave to stand for 30 minutes. Add the molasses, salt, and dissolved yeast. Add enough of the flour to make a soft dough. Put the dough into a buttered bowl, cover, and leave to rise until double. Turn out on a floured board and knead until elastic, about 10 minutes.

Divide into three loaves and place in 9-inch loaf pans and let rise again. Brush the tops with melted butter and bake in a 400°F, gas 6, oven for 40 to 50 minutes or until golden brown.

Variation: Add 5–6 tablespoons honey, 5 oz raisins, and 5 oz chopped nuts before adding the flour.

Sourdough Oat Bread

1 pint water	3 tablespoons honey
6 oz oats	1½ oz margarine or butter,
2 tablespoons honey	melted
½ lb unbleached flour	2 teaspoons salt
1½ cups Sourdough Starter	½ lb gluten and/or
(see page 84)	unbleached flour
¼ oz dry yeast	¾ lb whole-wheat flour

To make sponge: Pour ¾ pint boiling water over the oats and
let it stand until lukewarm. Stir in 2 tablespoons of honey, ½ lb
unbleached flour, and the starter. Blend thoroughly, cover the
bowl, and let stand for several hours, or in a cold room overnight.

When the sponge is ready, dissolve the yeast in ¼ pint warm
water and add to the sponge with the rest of the ingredients.
Blend well and turn out on a floured board. Knead, adding
more flour if necessary to make a firm, unsticky dough. Knead
until dough is smooth and elastic. Return to bowl; brush
dough with melted butter, cover, and let rise until double.

When dough is double, turn out on a floured board and
knead it down. Then cut into three pieces and shape into three
loaves. Place in buttered loaf pans, cover, and let rise until
double. Bake in a 350°F, gas 4, oven for 45 to 55 minutes.
After loaves are golden brown, brush them with butter. Turn
out on racks to cool. This bread makes wonderful toast.

Egg Bread

½ pint milk
2 oz butter or margarine
2 teaspoons salt
½ oz dry yeast

¼ pint lukewarm water
2 eggs, beaten
2 lb unbleached, sifted flour,
  approximately

Scald milk and add butter. Let cool. Add salt. Dissolve the yeast in the lukewarm water and let stand until it bubbles, about 5 minutes. Add the yeast and the eggs to the cooled milk. Gradually add the flour, beating it in thoroughly. Do not add any more flour than is necessary to make an easily handled dough, as the bread should be light and tender. Knead until smooth and elastic. Place in a greased bowl, cover, and let rise until double. Punch down and knead again.

Shape into loaves and place in 3 greased loaf pans. Cover and let rise until dough reaches the top of the pans. Bake at 350°F, gas 4, for 40 minutes.

Variation: CINNAMON BREAD. Roll a portion of the dough 1 inch thick. Spread with melted margarine or butter and sprinkle with natural sugar and cinnamon. You may also add chopped nuts or raisins. Roll as for Swiss roll and place in a greased pan with the seam at the bottom. Let rise until double and bake as for Egg Bread.

Sourdough French Bread

½ pint water
2 tablespoons honey
2 tablespoons margarine
¼ oz dry yeast

1½ cups Sourdough Starter
  (see page 84)
10 oz unbleached flour
2 teaspoons salt

Mix hot water, honey, and margarine. Cool to lukewarm. Add yeast, starter, and enough flour to make a firm dough (about ½ lb). Turn out on to a floured board and knead thoroughly. Place in a greased bowl, cover, and let rise until double. Punch dough down and let rise another 30 minutes.

Turn the dough out on to a floured board and let rest for 10 minutes before shaping. You may make a round loaf, a long thin loaf, or an oval loaf. Place on a baking sheet sprinkled with cornmeal. Let rise until double and bake at 400°F, gas 6, approximately 50 minutes.

The dough is usually slashed in several places with a very sharp knife just before baking. If a very sharp knife is used, the bread will not fall.

To make Egg-White Glaze: The best glaze for any hard-crusted bread is an egg white beaten just to blend with 1 tablespoon cold water. Brush this on the bread several times while baking.

Variation: This recipe can also be used to make 12 rolls. Shape the rolls after the first rising and place them on greased, cornmeal-sprinkled sheets. Cover and let rise again until double. Bake in a 400°F, gas 6, oven for 20 minutes, or until brown.

Swedish Rye Bread

½ pint scalded milk	¼ oz dry yeast
2½ teaspoons salt	14 oz unbleached flour, sifted
2 tablespoons molasses	1 tablespoon caraway seeds
2 tablespoons oil	8 oz rye flour
¼ pint water	

Pour the milk over the salt, molasses, and oil. Add the water. When cool, add the yeast and unbleached flour and beat until smooth. Stir in the caraway seeds. Gradually add the rye flour and mix to make a medium-stiff dough. The dough will be sticky. Turn it out on to a floured board and knead until smooth, about 10 minutes. Place in a buttered bowl, cover, and let rise until double, about 2 hours. Punch down and let rise again.

Turn out and shape into 2 oblong loaves. Place on buttered baking sheets that have been sprinkled with cornmeal. Let rise until double. Bake in a 375°F, gas 5, oven for 30 to 40 minutes.

Shepherds Bread

To make sponge:

1 package ($\frac{1}{4}$ oz) dry yeast	8 oz whole-wheat and 4 oz
$\frac{3}{4}$ pint lukewarm water	gluten and/or unbleached
2 tablespoons malt or honey	flour

Dissolve the yeast slowly in the water, and thoroughly blend in the flour and malt or honey. Cover with a clean towel and let rise in a warm place for approximately 4 hours.

To make dough:

1 package ($\frac{1}{4}$ oz) dry yeast	2 tablespoons oil
8 fl oz lukewarm water	8 oz gluten and/or unbleached
1 tablespoon salt	flour
2 tablespoons honey	4 oz whole-wheat flour

Dissolve the yeast in the water. Blend in the salt, honey, oil, and flour. Blend well. Thoroughly mix this into the sponge until pliable and smooth. Dough will pull away from the bowl. Turn out on a lightly floured board and knead for 3 to 5 minutes, and then let rest for 10 minutes.

Shape into one long or round loaf, cut a cross in the centre, and place on a cornmeal-sprinkled baking sheet. Cover and let rise until *almost* double. Then put a pan of boiling water on the floor of the oven and place the bread in the oven. Set temperature for 400°F, gas 6, and bake the bread for 45 minutes or until it is golden brown and done. Brush with Egg-White Glaze (see page 82) before and after baking.

Anadama Bread

½ pint scalded milk	2 teaspoons salt
½ pint water	½ oz dry yeast
4 oz yellow cornmeal	½ lb gluten and/or
3 tablespoons oil	unbleached flour
6 tablespoons molasses	1 lb whole-wheat flour

Combine the hot milk and ¼ pint boiling water and slowly add the cornmeal. Add the oil, molasses, and salt. Let stand until lukewarm. Sprinkle the yeast into ¼ pint warm water and let stand until it bubbles, about 5 minutes. Stir it into the cornmeal mixture. Beat in the flour. Turn out on to a floured board and knead until smooth and elastic, about 8 minutes.

Place dough in a greased bowl, cover, and let rise until double, about 1½ hours. Knead again and divide into 2 loaves. Place in buttered loaf pans, cover, and let rise until double again. Bake at 375°F, gas 5, for 40 to 50 minutes.

Sourdough Starter

Sourdough starters may also be purchased.

¼ oz dry yeast	¾ pint warm potato water
1 teaspoon natural sugar	(water in which potatoes have been cooked)

Combine all the ingredients and place in glass container.

Cover with cheesecloth and let stand at room temperature for 48 hours. You will need to stir it down occasionally.

After designated time, make sponge starter by adding equal parts of water and flour and letting it sit overnight in a warm place. Before adding any other ingredient, take at least 1 cup of sponge starter and store, covered, in the refrigerator. Then proceed with whatever recipe you are using.

QUICK BREADS

Stir batter only to moisten all the ingredients. Do not beat or knead quick breads. We think soy flour works well in muffins.

Walnut Bran Muffins

4 oz whole-wheat flour	3 tablespoons oil
⅛ teaspoon salt	1 egg
3 tablespoons non-fat, powdered milk	5 oz raisins (optional)
	4 tablespoons honey
3 teaspoons baking powder	8 fl oz milk
4 oz bran	4 oz walnuts

Sift together the flour, salt, powdered milk, and baking powder. Add and stir until mixed (but do not overmix) the remaining ingredients. Bake at 400°F, gas 6, for 15 minutes. Makes 12 muffins.

Wheat Germ Muffins

4 oz gluten and/or unbleached flour	2 tablespoons honey
	8 fl oz milk
4 oz whole-wheat flour	4 tablespoons vegetable oil
3 teaspoons baking powder	1 egg
½ teaspoon salt	2 oz wheat germ

Mix dry ingredients (except wheat germ) together. Mix moist ingredients together and stir into dry ingredients. Add wheat germ last. Bake at 350°F, gas 4, for 20 minutes in greased muffin tins. Makes 12 muffins.

Mexican Spoon Bread

1 small can creamed corn	2 teaspoons baking powder
¼ pint milk	½ teaspoon salt
4 tablespoons oil	4 oz mild green chilies,
2 eggs, slightly beaten	chopped
4 oz cornmeal	6 oz Cheddar cheese, grated

Mix together creamed corn, milk, oil, and eggs. Add cornmeal, baking powder, and salt. Pour half of the batter into a 9 × 9-inch baking dish. Place on top a layer made of half of the chilies and cheese. Pour on remaining batter. Top with the other half of chilies and cheese. Bake about 45 to 55 minutes at 350°F, gas 4.

Pumpkin Bread

1 large can pumpkin	6 teaspoons baking powder
1 pint honey	4 teaspoons cloves
8 fl oz oil	1 teaspoon cinnamon
2 eggs	½ teaspoon salt
10 oz whole-wheat flour, sifted	8 fl oz water
	10 oz chopped nuts
10 oz unbleached flour, sifted	10 oz raisins (optional)

Mix together pumpkin, honey, oil, eggs. Add dry ingredients alternately with water. Add nuts, and raisins if desired. Bake 1 hour at 350°F, gas 4, in 3 loaf pans.

Whole-Wheat Banana Nut Bread

4 tablespoons honey	6 oz whole-wheat flour
6 tablespoons oil	2 oz wheat germ
3 medium-sized, ripe bananas, mashed	2 teaspoons baking powder
	$\frac{1}{2}$ teaspoon salt
1 teaspoon vanilla	$\frac{1}{2}$ teaspoon cinnamon
2 eggs, well beaten	3 oz coarsely cut nuts

Cream honey and oil, and stir in bananas, vanilla, and well-beaten eggs. Combine all the rest of the ingredients and stir in only just mixed. Bake in 5 × 9-inch bread pan in 325°F, gas 3, oven for 1 hour and 10 minutes, or until golden brown.

Corn Bread

4 oz cornmeal	2 teaspoons baking powder
4 oz unbleached flour	2 eggs
4 tablespoons wheat germ	12 fl oz buttermilk
2 tablespoons rice polish	1 tablespoon honey
1 teaspoon salt	3 tablespoons oil

Mix dry ingredients together. Add beaten eggs to buttermilk, honey, and oil and mix together. Mix liquids into the dry ingredients until just moistened. Bake in an 8 × 8 × 2-inch cake pan at 425°F, gas 7, for 30 to 35 minutes.

Whole-Wheat Tortillas

$\frac{1}{2}$ lb whole-wheat flour	6 to 8 fl oz water
$\frac{1}{2}$ teaspoon salt	

Blend flour and salt. Stir in enough water to make a stiff

dough. Knead on a floured surface until smooth and elastic. Break dough into 1-inch rounds and roll into very thin tortillas. Cook over a low heat on a lightly greased griddle or frying pan. Turn one or more times. Makes 18 to 20, depending on size.

Wheat Germ Pancakes

12 fl oz milk
2 eggs
½ lb gluten flour

¼ lb wheat germ
1 teaspoon baking powder
1 teaspoon salt

Add milk and eggs to dry ingredients. Mix only until all ingredients are moistened. Bake on a hot griddle.

Sourdough Waffles

1 cup Sourdough Starter (see page 84)
¾ pint water
½ lb flour (⅓ soy flour, ⅓ whole-wheat flour, ⅓ gluten flour recommended)

4 tablespoons vegetable oil
3 tablespoons milk
1 teaspoon salt
1 teaspoon honey
2 eggs, separated

The night before, mix the Sourdough Starter, the water, and the flour. Reserve, the next morning, 1 cup of this mixture as future starter and store in the refrigerator. Add the rest of the ingredients to the remaining sourdough mixture, making sure that the egg whites are stiff-beaten and added last. Spoon the batter on to a waffle iron and bake until golden brown.

Variation: For pancakes cut the amount of oil in half.

Coffee Cake

5 oz whole-wheat flour*
1 oz wheat germ
3 teaspoons baking powder
¼ teaspoon salt
4 tablespoons honey
4 tablespoons oil
¼ pint milk
grated rind of ½ orange

6 tablespoons orange juice
1 egg, beaten
5 oz raisins
4 oz chopped nuts
1 teaspoon cinnamon
2 teaspoons butter
2 teaspoons natural sugar
(not honey)

Mix together the flour, wheat germ, baking powder, and salt. Mix together the rest of the ingredients except the cinnamon, butter, and sugar and add to the flour mixture. Pour the batter into a greased 9 × 13-inch cake pan. Mix the cinnamon, butter, and sugar; crumble and sprinkle over the top. Bake at 350°F, gas 4, for 20 to 30 minutes.

* See page 93 for a discussion of pastry and regular flours.

Desserts

Whole-wheat flour is available in some shops and all natural food stores. Flour texture varies greatly according to the mill source. For our pastry recipes we usually sift the flour twice, saving the chaff, or bran, for muffins and cookies, and using the sifted flour for pastry baking.

Most of the following recipes call for oil, although some ask for margarine or shortening. When buying shortening, read the labels for additives. Pure safflower oil shortening is available in natural food stores.

Generally our dessert recipes call for honey. As with breads, when substituting honey for sugar, always use one-third less honey than is specified for sugar.

Learn to use carob powder as a substitute for chocolate. Carob is much lower in starch and fat, and is richer in protein. It has a stronger flavour, so use less carob than chocolate.

A few of our recipes call for a springform (or tube) tin. They are preferable for shape and easy removal but not essential. We think an electric hand mixer is a good investment but an egg beater or wire whisk is usable with perseverance.

PIE CRUST. When making pie crust, blend shortening and flour well before adding cold water. Work very lightly after adding water, and roll with strong strokes.

BISCUITS. Biscuits gain nutritional value when extra powdered milk is added, but they brown quickly and should be baked at a slightly lower temperature than required in the recipe. Experiment in biscuit recipes with seeds, nuts, grains, unsweetened coconut, carob powder, and fruit.

CAKES. In making cakes, the leavening is crucial. If you don't use baking powder, 1½ to 2 tablespoons dry yeast is advised, although yeast is much less effective in cakes calling for a minimum of flour. Also, along with yeast, it is advisable to add any extra egg whites you may have. Beat them stiffly and fold in last. When using honey in cakes, bake at a slightly lower temperature to ensure complete baking in the centre.

Spring Rhubarb Pudding

8 slices toast	½ teaspoon cinnamon
12 fl oz milk	¼ teaspoon salt
1 oz butter	1½ lb diced rhubarb
5 eggs, slightly beaten	3 oz wheat germ
1 cup honey, or 6 oz natural sugar	

Trim crusts from toast and cut into ½-inch cubes. Place in a buttered casserole dish. Scald milk and add butter, stirring until melted. Pour over toast cubes and allow to stand 15 minutes. Combine eggs, honey, cinnamon, salt, and rhubarb. Stir into bread mixture. Sprinkle top with wheat germ. Bake 45 to 50 minutes. While warm, spoon into serving dishes and top with single cream. Serves 8 to 10.

Old-Fashioned Baked Custard

1½ pints milk
1½ teaspoons vanilla
pinch of salt
3 egg yolks

2 whole eggs
4–6 tablespoons honey, to
    taste
nutmeg

Place all the ingredients except nutmeg in blender and mix well. Pour into ungreased individual custard cups. Sprinkle with nutmeg. Set the dishes in a pan of warm water in the oven. Bake at 300°F, gas 1, until set, or when able to cut cleanly with a knife, approximately 1 hour.

Tapioca Pudding

8 tablespoons real tapioca
    (not large pearl)
1¼ pints milk

2 tablespoons honey
1 teaspoon vanilla

Soak tapioca in milk for 15 minutes. Cook over medium heat until thickened (8 to 10 minutes) without overcooking. Add honey and vanilla. Fresh fruit or coconut is optional. For a fluffier pudding, after removing from the heat, fold in one stiffly beaten egg white. Serves 4 to 6.

Whole-Wheat Pie Crust

4 oz whole-wheat pastry
    flour, sifted
4 oz unbleached flour

3 oz shortening
¾ teaspoon salt
3 or 4 teaspoons cold water

Blend the flours and shortening. Add salt and cold water and mix, with a minimum of strokes. Press into a ball and divide into two pieces and roll out. Place in greased pie tins and bake at 350°F, gas 4, for 15 minutes. Watch so they don't burn.

Danish Apple Pie

6 or 7 apples, sliced
6 tablespoons honey
2 oz margarine
6 oz whole-wheat flour

pinch of salt
1 teaspoon cinnamon
2 oz natural sugar

Butter a baking dish. Place the apples in the dish and drizzle with honey. Mix together margarine, flour, salt, cinnamon, and sugar. Sprinkle over the apples and bake at 375°F, gas 5, for 30 minutes.

Lemon Cheesecake

4 oz egg rusk crumbs
1 oz melted butter
9 tablespoons honey
1 large carton cottage cheese
4 eggs, separated
¼ teaspoon salt

1 teaspoon grated lemon peel
2 tablespoons lemon juice
1 teaspoon vanilla
1 carton unflavoured yogurt
(see page 42)

Mix together crumbs, butter, and 2 tablespoons honey with a pastry blender. Save aside 2 tablespoons of the mixture. Press remainder into bottom and ¾ way up the sides of a 10-inch springform tin, lightly greased. Bake 5 minutes at 250°F, gas ½.

In blender, combine cottage cheese, 3 tablespoons honey, egg yolks, salt, lemon peel and juice, vanilla, and yogurt. Blend until smooth.

Beat egg whites until soft peaks form, and then gradually add the 4 tablespoons of honey. Beat until stiff. Fold into the cheese mixture, mixing until smooth. Pour into the crust. Sprinkle over the set-aside crumb mixture. Bake at 250°F, gas ½ for 1 hour. Turn off heat and leave in the oven 1 more hour. Remove and cool thoroughly, and then chill overnight.

Strawberry Pie

1½ lb strawberries, cleaned and drained
3 tablespoons arrowroot
8 tablespoons honey
6 tablespoons boiling water

1 baked 8-inch pie shell (see page 95)
¼ pint cream, whipped and sweetened

Sort berries, reserving the larger ones. Mash the small berries to make 1 cup. Blend arrowroot, honey, and crushed berries in a small saucepan. Add boiling water and cook, stirring constantly, over medium heat until thickened and clear. Cool. Place whole berries in pie shell and pour the cooked strawberry mixture over them. Chill and serve with whipped cream.

Apple Pie

3 lb peeled and quartered apples
½ teaspoon nutmeg
9 tablespoons honey
½ lb whole-wheat pastry flour

1 unbaked pie shell (see page 95)
3 tablespoons lemon juice
2 tablespoons butter

Mix apples, nutmeg, 6 tablespoons honey, and 2 tablespoons flour together well and place in pie shell. Pour lemon juice over all. Blend remaining ingredients together and sprinkle over the apple mixture. Bake at 425°F, gas 7, for 1 hour.

Peanut Butter Biscuits

6 tablespoons oil
9 tablespoons honey
1 egg
2 oz non-hydrogenated
  peanut butter
6 oz sifted whole-wheat flour

1 teaspoon baking powder
½ teaspoon salt
1½ teaspoons orange juice or
  water
1 teaspoon vanilla

Mix oil, honey, and egg thoroughly. Blend in peanut butter. Mix in flour, baking powder, and salt alternately with orange juice or water. Add vanilla. Shape into small balls and flatten with a fork dipped in flour. Then bake on a greased baking sheet at 350°F, gas 4, for 10 minutes.

Oatmeal Biscuits

3 oz shortening
8 tablespoons honey
2 eggs
2 teaspoons vanilla
½ teaspoon salt
4 oz whole-wheat flour

2 teaspoons baking powder
12 oz oatmeal
2 oz nuts
2 oz shredded, unsweetened
  coconut

Cream shortening, honey, eggs, and vanilla together. Add salt, flour, baking powder, and oatmeal. Mix well. Add nuts and coconut and mix thoroughly. Drop by rounded teaspoons on greased baking sheet. Bake at 325°F, gas 3, for 10 minutes.

Variation : Add grated carrots, apples, or any seeds, especially poppy seeds. Cut-up dried fruits may also be added.

Crunchy Nut Biscuits

6 tablespoons honey
2 oz shortening
2 eggs
1 teaspoon vanilla

2 teaspoons baking powder
½ teaspoon salt
10 oz whole-wheat flour
5 oz chopped nuts

Preheat oven to 375°F, gas 5. Mix honey, shortening, eggs, and vanilla thoroughly. Add baking powder, salt, and flour and mix well. Stir in nuts. Shape dough into small balls. Place on ungreased baking sheet and flatten with bottom of a greased glass dipped in natural sugar. Bake 8 to 10 minutes. Makes 5 dozen.

Sour Cream Biscuits

12 tablespoons honey
4 oz shortening or butter
1 egg
1 tablespoon grated lemon
  peel

8 fl oz sour cream
1 teaspoon salt
1½ teaspoons baking powder
14 oz unbleached flour
nuts or raisins

Mix honey and shortening. Add egg and lemon peel and mix well. Mix in sour cream. Add salt, baking powder, and flour and mix thoroughly. Drop by rounded teaspoons on ungreased tin. Flatten with glass dipped in natural sugar. Press in nuts or raisins. Bake at 375°F, gas 5. Makes 7 dozen.

Sunflower Seed Walnut Bars

12 fl oz oil
12 fl oz honey
6 eggs
4 teaspoons baking powder
1½ lb sifted whole-wheat flour
drop of vanilla

2 tablespoons grated orange rind
4 tablespoons orange juice
2 oz shredded, unsweetened coconut
2 oz sunflower seeds
2 oz chopped walnuts

To make the bottom layer, mix half the oil, 4 fl oz honey, 2 eggs, 2 teaspoons baking powder, half the flour, and the vanilla together and pat into a greased 9 × 13-inch tin.

For the topping, beat the 4 eggs, mix them in with the remaining ingredients, and pour over bottom layer. Bake at 325°F, gas 3, for approximately 45 minutes. Cool and cut into squares.

Ranger Biscuits

2 oz shortening
12 tablespoons honey
1 egg
½ teaspoon vanilla
¼ teaspoon salt
1 teaspoon baking powder

2 oz shredded, unsweetened coconut
4 oz whole-wheat flour
4 oz oats
4 oz dry cereal flakes

Preheat oven to 350°F, gas 4. Mix shortening thoroughly with honey, egg, and vanilla. Stir in remaining ingredients. Drop by rounded teaspoons 2 inches apart on a greased baking sheet. Bake 10 minutes and remove from the sheet immediately. Makes 3 dozen.

Sesame Seed Biscuits

3 oz butter or margarine
9 tablespoons honey
2 eggs
1 teaspoon vanilla

6 oz unbleached flour
½ teaspoon baking powder
2 oz sesame seeds, toasted

Thoroughly mix together butter, honey, and eggs. Add vanilla and mix again. Add all the remaining ingredients and mix well. Drop by rounded teaspoons on a greased baking sheet. The biscuits will spread, so allow space between them. Bake at 325°F, gas 3, for 10 to 15 minutes.

Gingersnaps

6 oz shortening
a good ½ pint honey
2 eggs
6 tablespoons molasses
pinch of salt
8 oz whole-wheat flour

8 oz unbleached flour
2½ teaspoons baking powder
2 teaspoons each of cinnamon, powdered cloves, and ginger

Cream shortening, honey, and eggs. Add molasses and mix well. Add dry ingredients little by little, mixing after each addition. Roll in balls and flatten with a fork. Place on ungreased baking sheet and bake at 350°F, gas 4, for about 8 to 10 minutes, or until the bicuits are flat, cracked, and browned.

Delicious Squares

1 lb oats
4 oz sesame seeds
4 oz shredded, unsweetened
  coconut
2 oz wheat germ
2 oz nuts

dash of salt
¾ pint oil
5 or 6 eggs
12 tablespoons honey, or 8 oz
  natural sugar
1 teaspoon vanilla

Mix oats, seeds, coconut, wheat germ, nuts, and salt together and spread in bottom of a 9 × 13-inch baking tin. Mix together the oil, eggs, honey, and vanilla and pour over top of oat mixture. Bake at 350°F, gas 4, for 30 minutes. Cut into squares while warm.

Walnut Honey Cake

8 fl oz milk
9 tablespoons honey
6 oz whole-wheat flour,
  sifted
6 oz unbleached flour,
  sifted

1 teaspoon salt
2 teaspoons baking powder
2 oz chopped nuts
2 unbeaten egg yolks, or
  1 whole egg
1 oz butter, soft

Combine milk and honey in a large saucepan. Heat over medium heat, stirring constantly until mixed and lukewarm. Cool. Then, sift together flours, salt, and baking powder, and mix with the cooled honey and milk with an electric mixer at the lowest speed. (Can be mixed by hand.) Add nuts, egg, and butter and beat another 2 minutes at the lowest speed. Pour into 9 × 5 × 3-inch loaf tin, well greased on the bottom. Bake in 325°F, gas 3, oven approximately 1½ hours.

Poppy Seed Cake

6 oz poppy seeds	4 oz dry breadcrumbs
6 eggs, separated	2 teaspoons baking powder
12 tablespoons honey	$\frac{1}{4}$ teaspoon salt
$\frac{1}{4}$ pint vegetable oil	1 teaspoon vanilla

Cook poppy seeds in a pan with enough water to cover. Simmer for 15 to 20 minutes (watch water). Drain and cool. Beat egg whites until soft peaks form. Gradually add 3 tablespoons of honey. Continue beating until stiff. Set aside.

Beat the egg yolks until lemon coloured. Gradually beat in the remaining honey and then the oil. Add poppy seeds. Combine the bread crumbs, baking powder, and salt. Blend into the poppy-seed mixture. Lastly fold in the egg whites. Add vanilla.

Turn into greased 10-inch tube pan and bake at 325°F, gas 3, for 1 hour. Turn out to cool.

Fresh Carrot Cake

1 teaspoon cinnamon	4 large carrots, grated
1 teaspoon mace	3 teaspoons baking powder
$\frac{1}{2}$ teaspoon salt	4 oz sifted whole-wheat flour
4 oz butter or margarine	4 oz unbleached flour
$\frac{3}{4}$ pint honey	8 fl oz hot water
4 eggs	4 oz chopped nuts

Blend spices and butter. Gradually add honey and beat well. Beat in eggs one at a time and stir in carrots. Sift baking powder with flour, and add alternately with hot water. Add nuts and beat well. Put into a greased 9 × 13-inch tin; ice with Honey and Cream Cheese Icing (see page 107). Bake 35 minutes at 350°F, gas 4, or until done.

Gingerbread

9 tablespoons honey
9 tablespoons oil
12 tablespoons molasses
3 eggs
12 oz sifted whole-wheat flour

1 teaspoon salt
1½ teaspoons powdered cloves
3 teaspoons baking powder
1 teaspoon ginger
1½ teaspoons cinnamon
¾ pint milk

Mix honey, oil, molasses, and eggs together; set aside. Sift together all the dry ingredients. Add this flour mixture to the honey mixture alternately with the milk. Pour in greased 9 × 13-inch tin and bake at 350°F, gas 4, for 40 minutes.

Soy-Applesauce Cake

6 oz sifted whole-wheat flour
3 oz soy flour
2 oz powdered skim milk
4 teaspoons baking powder
1 teaspoon salt
2 teaspoons cinnamon

8 tablespoons honey
6 tablespoons oil
4 eggs
9 tablespoons applesauce
2 oz wheat germ
5 oz raisins

Sift together dry ingredients, except wheat germ. Cream honey, oil, and eggs together. Mix dry ingredients with the creamed mixture alternately with the applesauce, wheat germ, and raisins. Beat well. Turn into a greased 9 × 13-inch cake tin and bake at 350°F, gas 4, for 40 to 45 minutes.

Apple Spice Cake

2 oz butter
8 tablespoons honey
4 tablespoons cold coffee
1 egg, beaten
4 oz whole-wheat flour, sifted
2 oz bran

2 oz gluten and/or unbleached flour
1 teaspoon cinnamon
½ teaspoon powdered cloves
3 teaspoons baking powder
2 apples, grated

Cream butter and honey. Add coffee, which has been mixed with the egg. Add the dry ingredients alternately with the grated apple. Pour in a greased, 8-inch-square tin and bake at 350°F, gas 4, for 15 minutes. Lower temperature to 300°F, gas 2, for 20 more minutes.

Variation: A sprinkling of 2 teaspoons of cinnamon mixed with 3 teaspoons of natural sugar is a good addition before baking. Raisins or nuts may be added. This is also good served warm as a coffee cake.

Sour Cream Pound Cake

4 oz butter
12 tablespoons honey
6 eggs
1 teaspoon almond extract

8 fl oz sour cream
12 oz unbleached flour, sifted
½ teaspoon salt
1 teaspoon baking powder

Cream butter and honey. Add eggs one at a time, beating well after each. Add almond extract and sour cream, again beating well. Add flour, salt, and baking powder and mix well. Place in a greased, floured springform tin. Bake at 325°F, gas 3, for 1 to 1½ hours. Test to make sure it is done. We mix the cake with an electric mixer, but you can use an egg-beater and energy.

Oat Cake

1 egg	8 oz oats, quick or rolled
4 tablespoons oil	4 oz wheat germ
6 tablespoons honey	2 teaspoons baking powder
4 oz whole-wheat flour, sifted	8 tablespoons orange juice
	1 teaspoon vanilla

Blend egg, oil, and honey. Mix in dry ingredients alternately with the juice and vanilla. Bake at 350°F, gas 4, for about 40 minutes in an 8-inch square tin. Frost with Honey and Cream Cheese Icing (see page 107).

Sherry Wine Cake

4 oz butter or margarine	1 teaspoon nutmeg
15 tablespoons honey	pinch of salt (optional)
6 oz gluten and/or unbleached flour	¼ pint oil
	6 tablespoons sherry
6 oz whole-wheat flour	5 oz almonds, or other nuts
3 teaspoons baking powder	6 egg whites, stiffly beaten

Cream the butter and honey together. Sift flour, baking powder, nutmeg, and a pinch of salt, if desired, three times. Mix flour into the butter and honey alternately with the oil and sherry. Add almonds and beat well. Carefully fold in stiffly beaten egg whites. Pour into a greased and floured springform tin. Bake in preheated 350°F, gas 4, oven for 1 hour, or until a toothpick comes out clean when inserted in the centre.

Note: We make this cake without nuts for a good plain cake.

Honey and Cream Cheese Icing

The following is a very good icing that may be used on any cake.

Blend honey and cream cheese until a desired consistency is reached.

Vanilla or almond or lemon extract may be added. Chopped walnuts and/or shredded coconut can be sprinkled on top after spreading the icing.

Sesame Seed Squares

6 tablespoons honey
2 oz non-hydrogenated
  peanut butter
4 oz powdered milk

2 oz shredded, unsweetened
  coconut
4 oz sesame seeds

Heat honey and peanut butter. Add dry milk, coconut, and then seeds. Mix and pat into square tin. Refrigerate to set. Cut into squares.

Super Fudge

12 tablespoons honey
4 oz non-hydrogenated
  peanut butter
4 oz carob powder
4 oz sesame seeds

4 oz sunflower seeds
2 oz shredded, unsweetened
  coconut
2 oz dates or other fruit

Heat honey and peanut butter. Quickly add carob powder and
then all the seeds, coconut, and fruit. Pour into square pan and
refrigerate to harden. Cut into squares. Keep in the refrigerator
if possible.

Natural Health Candy

½ lb dates
1 lb dried figs
10 oz chopped walnuts
2 oz seedless raisins
1 lb dried apricots

1 teaspoon grated orange
  rind, sesame seeds, or
  shredded, unsweetened
  coconut

Put all ingredients, except rind, seeds, or coconut, through
food grinder. Mix well. Press into buttered dish and cut into
squares. Roll in rind, seeds, or coconut.

Index

More about Penguins and Pelicans

Penguinews, which appears every month, contains details of all the new books issued by Penguins as they are published. From time to time it is supplemented by *Penguins in Print*, which is a complete list of all available books published by Penguins. (There are well over four thousand of these.)

A specimen copy of *Penguinews* will be sent to you free on request, and you can become a subscriber for the price of the postage. For a year's issues (including the complete lists) please send 30p if you live in the United Kingdom, or 60p if you live elsewhere. Just write to Dept EP, Penguin Books Ltd, Harmondsworth, Middlesex, enclosing a cheque or postal order, and your name will be added to the mailing list.

Note: *Penguinews* and *Penguins in Print* are not available in the U.S.A. or Canada

Modern Vegetarian Cookery

Walter and Jenny Fliess

As founders and owners of the famous vegetarian Vega restaurants in Cologne and London, Walter and Jenny Fliess built up an international reputation for themselves many years ago.

In this cookbook they compressed a good slice of their life's work into some 500 recipes for soups, vegetarian dishes of all kinds, sauces, sweets, and uncooked meals. They are not directly concerned here with the broader theory of vegetarianism or food reform, and their book will simply and engagingly recommend itself to most readers as a very practical cookbook.

These fresh and imaginative recipes open up new culinary worlds and remove the sting from the injunction to 'eat plenty of fruit and vegetables'.

'Recipes to tempt even meat-eaters' – *Financial Times*

'500 recipes explain how to make everyday vegetables delicious and exciting' – *Vogue*

'The clearly set-out recipes are easy to follow . . . One could well live on vegetable fare' – *Tatler*

'A solid work of professional competence which many of our chefs might find intriguing' – *Culinarian* (U.S.A.)

'The idea that vegetarian cooking is necessarily dull is routed by the contents of this attractive book' – *House and Home* (South Africa)

The Last Whole Earth Catalog

Function

The *Whole Earth Catalog* functions as an evaluation and access device. With it, the user should know better what is worth getting and where and how to do the getting.

An item is listed in the *Catalog* if it is deemed:

(1) Useful as a tool,
(2) Relevant to independent education,
(3) High quality or low cost,
(4) Easily available by mail.

Catalog listings are continually revised according to the experience and suggestions of *Catalog* users and staff.

Purpose

We are as gods and might as well get good at it. So far remotely done power and glory – as via government, big business, formal education, church – has succeeded to the point where gross defects obscure actual gains. In response to this dilemma and to these gains a realm of intimate, personal power is developing – power of the individual to conduct his own education, find his own inspiration, shape his own environment, and share his adventure with whoever is interested. Tools that aid this process are sought and promoted by the *Whole Earth Catalog*.